STYLES

COMPENDIUM OF INTERIOR

© 2005 Assouline Publishing
601 West 26th Street, 18th floor
New York, NY 10001, USA
Tel.: 212 989-6810 Fax: 212 647-0005
www.assouline.com

Translated from the French by Sharon Grevet,
Molly Stevens, and Alison Dundy.

Color Separation: Gravor (Switzerland)
Printed by Grafiche Milani (Italy)

ISBN: 2 84323 720 3

FRANÇOIS BAUDOT

STYLES
COMPENDIUM OF INTERIOR

ASSOULINE

Contents

Stairs in the mansion of Bill Blass, Bedford, New York.

Styles

A distinctive manner of expression; a particular mode of living; a particular manner or technique by which something is done, created, or performed; a set of characteristics that enables a work to be classified with others into an aesthetic type. That is how the dictionary defines the word *style*.

That is precisely the goal of this book. It is not a substitute for a history of the decorative arts, but rather, through a series of period portraits, it characterizes some of the environments in which its contemporaries chose to live. Aside from dress, decor is the most immediate extension of the body; it constitutes a language, a set of signs, a definite notion of the art of living at a particular moment in time: "Tell me where you live and I'll tell you who you are." Taking that cliché a step further, we recognize that the sum of the information contained in a single space—designed, desired, or suffered by the individual who occupies it—constitutes a sort of DNA of infinite mystery: the story of a life. If our descendants were to indulge in the whim of deriving an equation from the bric-a-brac found in weekend flea markets, they would obtain a surprisingly accurate picture of the preferences of each generation going back a century or more.

Note that the concept of style also encompasses writing: literary expression, phraseology, execution, and attitude. "What is art?" asked André Malraux. "The way in which forms become style." A distinction has not always been made between decoration per se and architecture, since the latter is essentially defined by walls and their ornamentation. Le Brun was a painter, but he was nevertheless the great decorator of Versailles. But, in that respect, furnishings counted less

Library of the Château de Groussay, Montfort-l'Amaury.

than the layout of a site, its technical aspects, and the politics it reflected. Paintings, objects, costly fabrics, rugs, and tapestries, having no direct relation- ship with a place, were mere bystanders.

With the advent of furnishings in the late eighteenth century came the formation of coherent and indivisible wholes. Decorators and couturiers—masters of amuse- ment and the personal arts—soon followed. From that time on, fashion seized hold of taste and has never stopped controlling it.

Decoration, intrinsically, does not exist. There is only decor and decorators, a repertoire of forms and a catalog of needs. The development of the two is not linear. But at the risk of seeming discursive, it is nonetheless closely bound with the Zeitgeist.

Each of the following chapters treats one of the catalysts of a particular style. At the dawn of time, Cro-Magnon man decorated the walls of his cave. Today's student tacks a jumble of photographs to the walls of his dormitory room. Between these two extremes is a chain of countless stages in the voyage around a room. Louis XV loved rococo; the sweep of the airy curves that belied its melancholy pandered to his lasciviousness. But he was obliged to yield to the return of neoclassicism at the urging of his clever confidante, Madame de Pompadour, whose brother Marigny, the king's director of fine arts, was enthralled with the first archeological excavations at Pompeii. This interest in ancient revival spread throughout Europe, as the emperor Napoleon scoured the ornamental lexicon of the ancient Egyptians and Romans for an excuse for a new- found legitimacy.

In the nineteenth century, the exponential development of various industries and the simultaneous advent of new social classes wrought considerable change in the decorative landscape. They did so by launching the concept of decorative art, discarding the foundations of design, and prefiguring the consumer society that would blossom in America between the two World Wars and in Europe after the Liberation.

The twentieth century witnessed an acceleration of trends. Until then, the history of the decorative arts was divided—admittedly arbitrarily—into large slices that corresponded to reigns or movements, extending and intersecting over several decades. Beginning in the twentieth century, however, the figure of the creator would predominate. Many creators may be temporarily grouped under a collective label, but the fact remains that the singularity of each of them has left its mark. Often accompanied by imperious discourse, each underlies an elaborate style that breaks with those that preceded or rivaled it.

Two major categories stand out from this divergent mix. These two divisions are, moreover, found in most artistic disciplines in the contemporary world. On one side are the classics, and on the other, the moderns. An enduring dichotomy, in the field of interior architecture, this essentially translates into a clash between decorative artists and designers, between the work of skilled artisans, who hark back to a tradition of excellence, and the experimental spirit of innovative designers. In the name of functional beauty, the latter strive to develop forms intended for mass production, which are thus more affordable for the majority of consumers. The political convictions that have accompanied these two ethics—diametric opposites in every way for more than a century—now, at the dawn of the third millennium, seem somewhat trifling. Without suggesting that we have reached "the end of the story," with perspective we find that classics and moderns conflict about as often as they harmonize. For example, the industrial furnishings that engineer Jean Prouvé intended for public institutions are now sold as antiques. Inspired secondhand antique dealers offer antique bathtubs and four-poster canopy beds to generations whose forebears slept on straw. Thus, styles observe one another, grasp one another, and complement one another, which in profusion can create a confusion that exists purely on the surface. This illustrates the aphorism of the famous aesthete of decoration Carlos de Beistegui, who said, "In the thirties, I wanted my living room to resemble a bathroom. Today my bathrooms resemble living rooms."

Middle Ages

This period is marked by innovation and change, especially during the reign of Charles IV, who turned Paris into a center for the arts. Decorators and poets from the nineteenth century did the rest.

The Middle Ages constitute a sort of prehistory of the decorative arts, a period of time between antiquity and the modern world, characterized by Gothic architecture. The invaluable remnants of medieval times, namely cathedrals and castles, were constantly reinterpreted, allowing for every kind of fantasy, and kept alive largely by the pride of a nobility that derived its legitimacy from chivalrous romances, tales of courtly love, and fairy tales—an imagery that has

Anonymous, *Portrait of Jean Bedford,* c. 1440. Gold-enameled medallion, Schatzkammer, Munich.

OPPOSITE: Christine Pisan, *Master of the Cité des Dames,* 1410–1412. Illumination. British Library, London.

been romanticized by the historicism of the nineteenth century. From the early Carolingian Renaissance (an early phase of the Romanesque, beginning in the eighth century) through the twelfth century, domestic decor differed little from religious decor. Thus, based on the type of its ecclesiastic structure, the High Renaissance was divided into two distinct sections: the Romanesque period and the Gothic period. While they are often contrasted, these styles also coexisted for different purposes.

Concurrent with the great feudal estates and monastic powers, with castle keeps and rural bell towers, the Romanesque style is identified by its barrel vaults and its ornamental repertoire, with

origins in Greco-Roman, Byzantine, Celtic, or even Iberian Islamic antiquity, naively reinterpreted. Grand sculpted decors adorned with imaginary bestiaries occupy the key points of geometric architectural forms. Decorative plates, ivories, miniatures, religious articles, and fabrics in particular counted for more than furniture, which was rough and crude, in those interiors where prayer and even miracles seemed the only remedies to the darkness and cold.

Initiated in the mid-twelfth century, Gothic art is characterized by its ribbed vaults. Tapered more or less, depending on the distance between the center points, and reinforced by fine, powerful ribs, the vaults reached unprecedented heights. Self-supporting walls

In Gothic-era interiors, the chimney and the bed were central elements. There was no symmetry. Practical aspects were prioritized; the tile floor was accommodating for dogs and dirt tracked in from outside.

adorned with polychrome stained-glass windows let in a profusion of light. The Gothic style spread; it escalated and proliferated. Where Romanesque art bowed down, Gothic reigned. While one humbly assimilated with a nature still wild and feared, the other asserted itself as an urban style. The kings of France were crowned beneath the ogees of Reims Cathedral while their widows retired to the silence of Romanesque abbeys. Of their castles and dwellings, today only a few ruins remain. Unless seasoned by the restorations of architects keen on historical interpretation, they became more eloquently suggestive of an infatuation with medievalism than of the Middle Ages themselves. Furniture was still a rare thing in these interiors, and the aristocracy, who traveled extensively, took their furnishings with them when they visited their vast estates and their relations. Thus chests, which served as both luggage and seating, remain the furnishing most symbolic of the Middle Ages. Decoration often included the painting of coats of arms on wood-paneled walls or colorful painted wood ceilings. Another invaluable signature of the period were wool tapestries, also transported, that were used to warm the walls of common rooms and to serve as decoration. Often, benches and cabinets were built into the architecture, eliminating the need for furnishings, save the occasional table, bed, or stool. Time at home was spent around massive fireplaces or by window openings. The floors were warmed with crude braided mats where hunting and watch dogs slept. Intermittently, the echoes of battle could be heard in the distance. In 1384 and the ensuing years, the plague and its countless deaths would accompany the Hundred Years War. Still, those years of unrest were interspersed with periods of peace, whose prosperity promoted the art of living. This was particularly true under the reign of Charles VI (1368–1422) of France. Though he is primarily remembered for his mental illness, under his monarchy France nevertheless experienced more than twenty years of reprieve. There was an influx of artists and artisans, whose livelihood depended on a court that possessed great wealth and was eager to display it. The subsequent upheavals left little evidence of this splendor, which heralded the Renaissance. Yet *The Very Rich Hours of the Duke of Berry,* artwork commissioned by Queen Isabeau of Bavaria, ceremonial weaponry, and especially, the gold-enameled objects bear witness to a high level of refinement. Once France had been pacified and unified through the tireless efforts of Louis XI, Charles VIII and Louis XII opened up to the allure of the Italian style. An entire sensibility was thereby transformed.

Notre-Dame "Goldnes Roddle" (Golden Horse), 1404. Enamel, chiseled gold, sapphires, rubies, pearls. National Museum of Bavaria, Altotting.

OPPOSITE: Folding table, c. 1500. Wood, Musée National du Moyen-Âge, Paris.

A magnificent gift from Isabeau of Bavaria to her husband, Charles VI, in 1405, this unusual piece represents the sophisticated and technically perfect work executed by the goldsmiths who worked in the French courts at the end of the Middle Ages.

Renaissance

The beginning of modern times, the Renaissance extended from Quattrocento Italy to the end of the sixteenth century in Flanders. It was a time of humanism and the great return of the Greco-Roman artistic canon. The style is essentially European.

If there is one distinctive sign of the transition from the Middle Ages to the years of the Renaissance, it is the rise of humanism, the priority placed on the individual over the religious. Man, conceived in the image of God and his most beautiful creation, was returned to the center of the universe. The presence of great wealth and stable governments fueled progress and the presence of a will to learn

Giorgio Vasari, *Laurent de' Médicis (the Magnificent)*, 1550. Oil on wood. Gallery of the Offices, Florence.

OPPOSITE: Domenico Ghirlandaio, *Birth of St. John the Baptist*, fifteenth century. Fresco. Santa Maria Novella, Florence.

Castellano, *Studiolo*, 1476. Marquetry, Ducal Palace, Urbino.

An accomplished warrior depicted by Piero Della Francesca in his famous portrait, Federigo II Montefeltro, the duke of Urbino (1422–1482), was also a man of letters and a patron of the arts. It is said that he modeled for Baldassare Castiglione for his representation of The Courtier. *In this room, trompe l'oeil depicts still lifes inspired by intimist painting from northern Europe.*

A vase with a blood jasper cover and a gilded enamel base. Representing fifteenth-century Florentine taste, it belonged to the collection of Laurent the Magnificent in the Pitti Palace.

OPPOSITE: Alessandro Frei del Barbera, *La Bottega dell' orifice*. Palazzo Vecchio, Florence.

This painting, which hung in the Studiolo of the Grand Duke François de' Medici (1541–1587), depicts his artisans making some of the treasures that can be found today in the Pitti Palace in Florence.

Fontainbleau school,
*Gabrielle d'Estrées and one
of her sisters*, sixteenth
century. Oil on wood,
Louvre Museum, Paris.

OPPOSITE: High-back chayère,
with Henri II monogram,
mid-sixteenth century, wood.

*This kind of chair played an
important role in the history of
furniture, acting as a symbol of
power from the Middle Ages to
the seventeenth century. It was
meant mostly for priests, those
in power, and the elderly, and
pointed to their honorability.
Others would remain standing.
Similar to a throne, the chayère
was not about comfort. But, the
way in which it was adorned
matched its function.*

and achieve. In 1500, France was dreaming of Italian conquests. With curiosity and an agenda of expansionism, the slightest pretext was enough for its armies to wage war on the peninsula. But instead, in the end, it was Italy's charm and culture that conquered the French kings. Henri VIII, Louis XII, and then Francis I transported new Italian refinements to the Loire Valley and Fontainebleau. During the sixteenth century, these objects prompted the flowering of a society that would welcome the art of landscape gardening in its villas, and ideas and dialogue in its towns.

Francis I (1494–1547), patron of the arts and conqueror of the battle of Marignan at age 20, remains the emblematic figure of the complex style that flourished at the crossroads of Europe, between the merchantile opulence of Flanders and the extraordinary aesthetic revolution in Tuscany nearly one hundred years earlier.

The homes of the wealthy no longer consisted solely of castles, but included palazzos and villas. Residences were now flooded with light, walls were adorned with frescoes, fireplaces were ornamented with mantels, floors of brick or tile often followed decorative, geometric patterns, and cushioned chairs began to replace benches and stools. Paintings of sensual women stood out against the stuccoes and furniture as a whole was more common, as were decorative carvings, inlays, and fabric drapes and coverings.

The Florentine Filippo Brunelleschi (1377–1446) was of the first artist/engineers who would influence the Renaissance. For his signature work, the dome of a Gothic Florentine cathedral (the Duomo), he staved off traditional influence, applying to the colossal edifice and its dome lessons from his studies of the proportions and style of the ruins of ancient Rome. This was no stylistic imitation, but rather a return to classicism that would result in unprecedented forms and beauty. With innovative engineering, Brunelleschi constructed the catherdral's dome without the presence of outside supports by using tension rings. His influence prevailed until the dawn of the twentieth century.

In that theory of the arts, whose golden age was embodied by
the Medici era, the concept of decorative art had no true meaning
yet, other than as part of art as a whole, encompassing painting,
sculpture, and especially architecture—the unifier of all ornamentation. In the Flemish countries, this reconquest of human reality
experienced its most graceful developments through decoration.
The richness of Dutch interiors, as depicted in numerous genre
paintings, illustrates family values and tasteful domesticity. Kettles
and Mason jars, oriental rugs imported through the Hanseatic
ports and heavy, gleaming furniture are reflected in eyelike
convex mirrors in those interior views and floral paintings, virtual

cameos of bourgeois felicity. Everything radiates order, cleanliness, and probity.

On the banks of the Arno, however, the contemporary interiors of Luca Della Robbia (1400–1482) or Ghirlandaio (1449–1494) reflect no such domesticity. In Italy, love of the arts and poetry coincided with a sense of grandeur, always tempered by a sense of humor and, therefore, exaggeration. Hence the exuberance in attitudes and etiquette. As for the dwellings themselves, their brightness, comfort, and harmony are the admiration of all the guests of the noble families that still occupy them. In addition to the often austere palaces within walled citadels, Florentines and Romans

Until the fifteenth century, this room acted as the heart of the château's living quarters. The lord would receive an audience in the anteroom known as the Chambre de Parade, which flanked his richly adorned bedroom. A fine lady would receive visitors lying down. The Chambre de Retrait, or semi-private chamber, was used for rest or personal matters. In both cases, the bedroom suite was the center of social life.

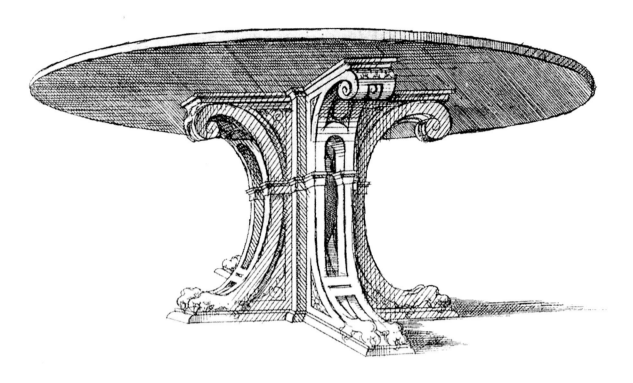

Jacques Androuet du Cerceau,
designs of three types of tables.

OPPOSITE: Walnut and ebony chair,
second half of the sixteenth century.
Collection of Barons Nathaniel
and Albert von Rothschild.

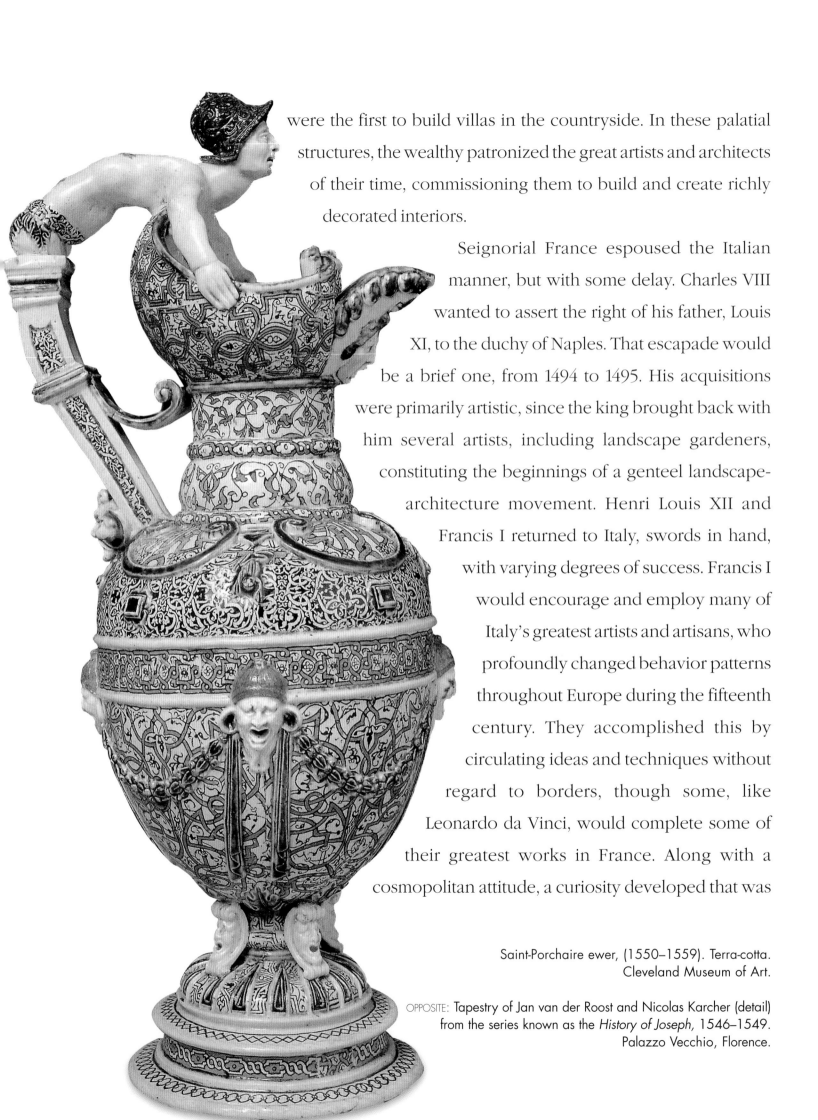

were the first to build villas in the countryside. In these palatial structures, the wealthy patronized the great artists and architects of their time, commissioning them to build and create richly decorated interiors.

Seignorial France espoused the Italian manner, but with some delay. Charles VIII wanted to assert the right of his father, Louis XI, to the duchy of Naples. That escapade would be a brief one, from 1494 to 1495. His acquisitions were primarily artistic, since the king brought back with him several artists, including landscape gardeners, constituting the beginnings of a genteel landscape-architecture movement. Henri Louis XII and Francis I returned to Italy, swords in hand, with varying degrees of success. Francis I would encourage and employ many of Italy's greatest artists and artisans, who profoundly changed behavior patterns throughout Europe during the fifteenth century. They accomplished this by circulating ideas and techniques without regard to borders, though some, like Leonardo da Vinci, would complete some of their greatest works in France. Along with a cosmopolitan attitude, a curiosity developed that was

Saint-Porchaire ewer, (1550–1559). Terra-cotta.
Cleveland Museum of Art.

OPPOSITE: Tapestry of Jan van der Roost and Nicolas Karcher (detail) from the series known as the *History of Joseph*, 1546–1549. Palazzo Vecchio, Florence.

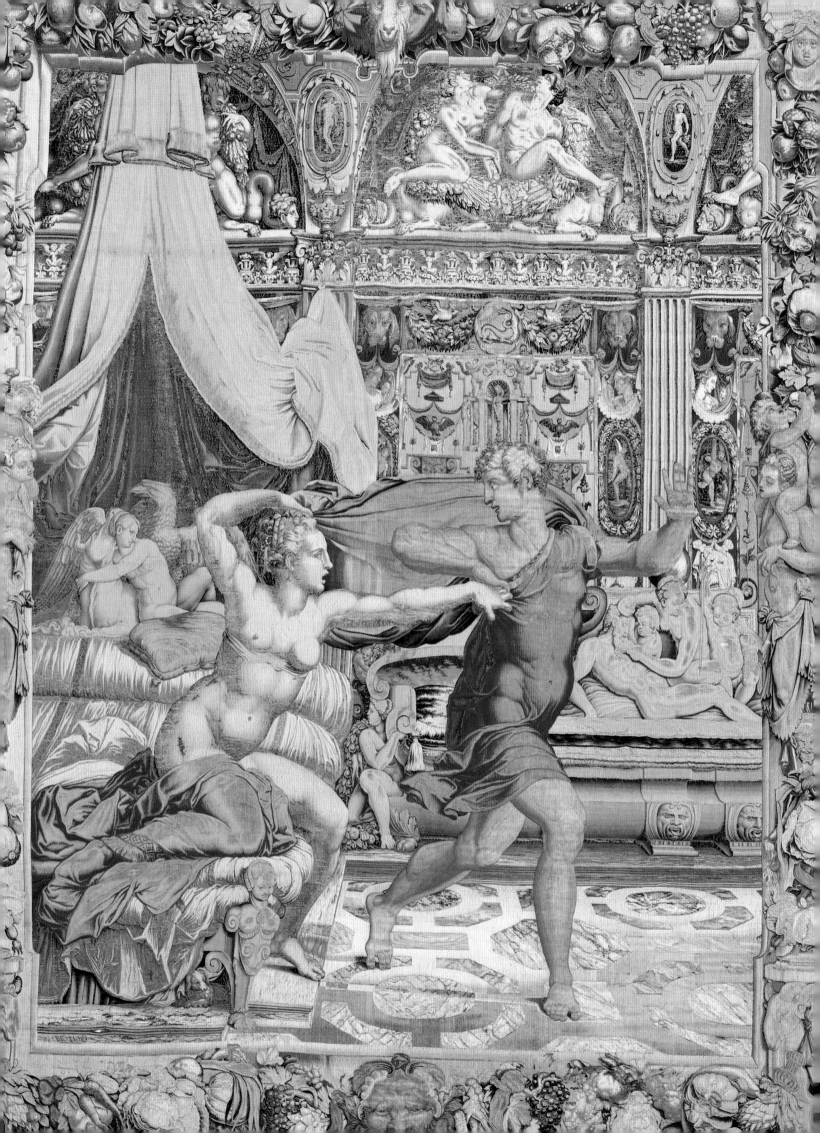

reflected, in the latter part of the Renaissance, through the concept of the tinkerer's workshop. The cosmic vision of the world at the time was one where enamel, stained glass, tapestries, mosaics, and earthenware coincided with various animal and vegetable monstrosities, and largely imaginary and otherworldly creatures.

But it is in its unprecedented, composite ornamentation that the northern Renaissance seems the most disconcerting. For both interiors and exteriors alike, ornamentation consisted of a combination of knot-work, leather, ova, amulets, fleurs-de-lis, and flying volutes, with coats of arms drawn from heraldry, a bestiary inherited from mythology or borrowed from fairy tales. From this point of view, in the collective imagination the period of the Renaissance remains largely a supernatural one.

Willem Claesz Heda, *Still Life on a Bare Table*, 1629.

PRECEDING PAGES:
Antiques closet in Rubens's house, 1609. Anvers, Belgium.

OPPOSITE: Pieter de Hooch, *La Bonne Ménagère*, c. 1650. Rijksmuseum, Amsterdam.

Bedroom, Rembrandt's
house, Amsterdam,
c. 1650.

*Rembrandt Harmensz Van
Rijn lived from 1639 to 1658
in a house in old Amsterdam,
which today bears his name.
Along with his studio, this
room was one of the most
beautiful in the house. He
painted Saskia here, whom he
married in 1694. She is
portrayed lying down,
exhausted after giving birth.
This drawing was recently used
to build a replica of the room
with its bed alcove.*

FOLLOWING PAGES:
Bartholomeus van Bassen,
Flemish interior, 1622.

Louis XIII

It is generally accepted that a golden age in the decorative arts flourished under the reign of this unassuming ruler. In a France impoverished by war, the lavish decor of Valois evolved into the magnificence of Versailles.

French school, *Cardinal Mazarin*, c. 1650. Oil on canvas. Versailles museum.

Born in Italy, sophisticated and politically shrewd, this Richelieu protégé headed the king's council after his death. At the same time, because of his great fortune he was able to purchase a huge collection and library that has since contributed to France's heritage.

OPPOSITE: Johan Georg Hinz, *Cupboard with precious objects*, c. 1630–1688. Château de Friedenstein.

The time of the Musketeers is to the history of France what the Western saga is to the conquest of the American West; it is a saga that is both political and aesthetic, where cruelty coincided with swashbuckling adventure, and exuberance with ingenuity. It was an interlude between the Renaissance and the Grand Siècle, a troubled period that nevertheless generated exceptional creativity. From 1610 to 1661, not a year passed when France was at peace, and yet the population flourished and Paris emerged unscathed. Those who ruled were exceptional personalities, and all the more uninhibited since Cardinal Richelieu, followed by his successor, Mazarin, had the enlightened support of Louis XIII, and then of his widow, the regent Anne of Austria. While Richelieu was hungry for glory, supported the humanities (he founded the

FOLLOWING PAGES:
LEFT: Abraham Bosse, *Banquet Hosted by Louis XIII for the New Knights of the Order of the Holy Spirit in the Fontainbleau Ballroom*, May 14, 1633. Engraving. Versailles museum.
RIGHT: Table set in the spirit of the seventeenth century, by Carlos de Beisteigui. c. 1950. Château de Groussay, Montfort-l'Amaury.

FROM LEFT TO RIGHT:
Mazarin bureau, Boulle marquetry, c. 1700. Red tor-
toiseshell inlays. Versailles
museum.

Abraham Bosse,
Allegory of the Sight,
c. 1630–1640. Gravure.

Mirror (said to be from
Maria de' Medici), c. 1630.
Enamel, gold, and precious
stones. Louvre Museum,
Paris.

Académie Française), and had only a tentative interest in the arts,
the commitment of the second prime minister and cardinal to the
arts was beyond doubt. After an impoverished childhood, the
Italian-born Cardinal Mazarin became a perpetual collector, a passion he passed on to his student Louis XIV. While Louis took pains
to engender a distinctly French style in the decorative arts and was
decidedly successful, the origin of his style was undeniably Italian,
if not Baroque. The Spanish-educated regent was all the more open
to the Romanesque climate, a quality that was instilled by the pro-
tector of her beloved son, whose birth she had awaited for twenty-
three years and whom she was preparing for glory.

In 1629, the fortification of any new construction was prohibited.

Richelieu's France followed suit in an elite economy from which decor greatly profited. As a result, the French provinces became dotted with those light brick and stone houses modeled after the Royal Palace in Paris (now the Place des Vosges) that continue to embody the halcyon lifestyle of a country gentleman.

In these residences with their finely painted beams, the floors were tiled with marble or terra-cotta. The furniture, which harked back to the previous century, was waxed and sparkled in the dusky light. On the walls, the greenery spun out those mysteries that stood against the Delft blues and whites, combined with the harmony of the parrot-like colors of the flatland tulips.

The Romanesque world of the nineteenth century did much to

Faithful depictions of aristocratic life in France in the seventeenth century, details from the intimist engravings by Abraham Bosse (1602–1676) provide precious information on the period. For example, the bed, when covered during the day, was like a fabric box richly decorated with trimmings.

confer consistency to what our antique dealers call Louis XIII style, although the king lived only forty-two years. This period ran from the end of the Valois period to the zenith of the Bourbon period—in other words, between two foreign regencies both infatuated with the decorative arts. In homes, the joyful polychromy of the paneling painted with warriors and beautiful ladies contrasted with the austerity of the large furnishings—furniture with secret compartments and woodwork encrusted with precious materials. The polished pewter reflected heavy pieces of plate. The fruits and vegetables of still lifes showcased a lifestyle that was domestic and calm.

In the early seventeenth century, other than a hall, a residence consisted of nothing more than a bedchamber. In that main room, a distinguished lady would receive her guests while reclining on her stately bed, *à la* Marquise de Rambouillet, exemplar of *les précieuses,* those well-read and refined ladies whom Molière ridiculed in his famous satire. Other than this enclosed space so conducive to all sorts of gallantries, the home consisted of only a gallery and toilets. Rooms with no designated function were ordered as needed; privacy had not yet been invented.

From the regency of Marie de' Medici to that of Anne of Austria, and from the ministry of Richelieu to that of Mazarin, the provinces became dotted with light brick and stone slate-roofed houses, inspired by the Royal Palace in Paris—midway between the big city and the country. Finely decorated with polychrome beams, the reception rooms had tiled floors, as illustrated by the engravings of Abraham Bosse. This quasi-rustic style was popular among the country aristocracy until the Revolution. At the dawn of the 1950s, it was reclaimed by the new French upper class, avid for legitimate but luxurious simplicity.

View of the Château de Vaux-le-Vicomte (Seine-et-Marne).

Nicolas Fouquet

Nicolas Fouquet was a visionary. In just a few years, he brought together the most talented artists for the Château de Vaux, laying the artistic groundwork for Louis XIV. The king never forgave Fouquet, but he did learn his lesson.

On August 24, 1661, young Louis XIV, who, at the age of 5, had ascended to the throne of a France impoverished by the Fronde (the rebellion of the nobility), inaugurated the new estate of his minister of finance, Nicolas Fouquet, with the entire court in attendance. The masterpiece of architect Louis Le Vau (1612–1670), the Château of Vaux-le-Vicomte located in the Seine-et-Marne region, was built with extreme speed in perfect harmony with the

surrounding gardens. In fact, the castle's integration into the landscape, which is still miraculously preserved, constituted its great novelty. With its interplay between rich interior decors, breathtaking views displayed through the high windows, an extension of the decor and its succession of reception rooms, Vaux-le-Vicomte is also a marvelous social complex that reflects the personality of its owner. This precursor of Versailles seems to have been a veritable revelation to the Sun King: he would later build a monument to his own glory. Refusing to occupy the apartment that his jubilant minister had decorated for him, the king withdrew, meditated, and came to a decision. Three weeks later, Fouquet was arrested and incarcerated for life after a biased trial in which he was charged with corruption. From that time onward, the king would govern by himself. To assert his absolute power, he also laid claim to the remarkable variety of artists with whom the minister had surrounded himself. In addition to Le Vau, who would oversee the first expansion of the Versailles Palace, the

Anonymous, *Salutary Reminder,*1662. Etching and burin engraving. Louvre Museum, Paris.

landscape designer Le Nôtre, and the painters Le Brun and Nicolas Poussin would be called upon to collaborate on the monarch's grand construction projects. The fact remains that the environment of Louis XIV's reign and its inseparable style were drafted during the course of one wild summer's day, one that would be long remembered by such independent thinkers as Madame de Sévigné, Mademoiselle de Scudéry, and Jean de La Fontaine—who wrote "Elegy to the Nymphs of Vaux," a distant echo of the enthusiasm that had once worked magic.

OPPOSITE: View of the garden from the antichamber of Hercules at the Château de Vaux-le-Vicomte.

Grand Siècle

In conceiving the formidable mecanics of Versailles, Louis XIV gave France an instrument of absolute power. The whole of Europe imitated the style that became a symbol of greatness, though it was one of the most modest.

Antoine Coysevox, *Louis XIV*.
Marble.
Versailles museum.

OPPOSITE: Room of the Abundance, in the Great Apartments of the Château de Versailles.

Decorated in 1680, this room was used for many years to display the Cabinet of Curiosities and other rare objects, before becoming the king's game room. The painting on the ceiling, Abundance and Liberality, *is a work by René-Antoine Houasse, depicting the most precious objects in the Cabinet around its circumference. The four bronze busts of the descendants of Louis XIV were part of ancient royal collections. To the right of the door are two portraits:* Louis of France, duke of Bourgogne *(1682–1712), painted by Hyacinthe Rigaud, and* Louis XV, king of France and Navarre *(1710–1774), by Jean-Baptiste van Loo.*

A great king, great battles, great buildings... Louis XIV, born in 1638, proclaimed himself absolute monarch as a young man, armed only with an awareness of royal grandeur. His dazzling sign would be emblematic of an entire century. To consolidate his power, the king (who would subjugate the great nobles) constructed an implacable mechanism whose outward representation was the Château de Versailles: more than a palace, it was a temple to the glory of this thoroughly hands-on prince. Costumes, decor, entertainment—during the seventeenth century, every form of artistic endeavor pointed to the king. All beauty, all glory, and all thought emanated from him, in an extension of his quasi-divine essence. As talented as they may have been, Racine and Lully, Bossuet and Le Brun, Mansart and Le Nôtre were no more than pieces in the gigantic puzzle that was the "century of Louis XIV."

FOLLOWING PAGES:
Model of the ambassadors' staircase, Château de Versailles.

He was the sovereign of the most populous and most powerful nation in Europe, and served as a model for other European kings. "A style is a development, a consistent set of forms united by mutual convenience," wrote Henri Focillon. From this point of view, the designers and decorators of Versailles—and other seats of power—proved indeed remarkably consistent under the leadership of a man who, in addition to being a great king, was also a remarkable art director, both in his official capacity and in his private life. The elements of the Louis XIV style espouse the curve of the king's own destiny, and carry in them the seeds of the inevitable evolution of the French monarchy. Royal at its zenith, this aesthetic propaganda—a token of the monarchy's own perception as an eternal, strong, and centralizing state—would have a lasting impact on the French subconscious. Order, classicism, symmetry, and an immoderate taste for grand perspectives tempered by reason remain relevant in a France that has changed little stylistically in three centuries.

OPPOSITE: Jacques Garcia, apartment decorated with furniture from the Louis XIV period, Paris.

ABOVE (FROM LEFT TO RIGHT): Over the resting bed, a portrait of Louis XVI by Mignard.

Ceiling painted by Le Brun; on the floor, a tapestry of the Savonnerie from the collection of Louis XIV.

Brussels tapestry by Van der Hooch and Teniers, 1680; seat of the Grand Dauphin and Boulle desk in wood marquetry.

In these rooms from the seventeenth century, the decorator replicated living quarters outside of Versailles that were occupied by aristocratic courtiers.

A period of transition between the Renaissance era and modern times, the century of Louis XIV, with its splendor and harmony, has proven difficult to re-create (except for a few interpretations in bourgeois interiors)—yet there has been no dearth of Latin American millionaires hunting down the ceremonial furnishings of the Grand Siècle.

Designers have surrounded themselves with remarkable collections inspired by André-Charles Boulle (1642–1732), the precursor of modern cabinetmaking, who was imitated by his four sons and then copiously copied under the Second Empire. And while one might say of a megalomaniac,

Louis XIV chair, seventeenth century. Sculpted and gilded wood. Louvre Museum, Paris.

"Who does he think he is, Louis XIV?" the less grandiose also describe their residences as a "little Versailles." But when all is said and done, building Versailles cost the French government no more than the price of an aircraft carrier. Today, no estate receives more visitors than Versailles, which is so miraculously preserved despite revolutions, pillaging, and the cost of operating it.

Nicolas de Largillière, *Madame de Ventadour with portraits of Louis XIV and his heirs*, c. 1715–1720. Oil on canvas. Wallace Collection, London.

OPPOSITE: Pierre Patel, *View of the house and park of Versailles*, 1663, Château de Versailles.

The palace of Louis XIV as it stood when Le Vau died. Mansart finished the project, enlarging it considerably. The king and the court moved there in 1682.

FOLLOWING PAGES: **Anonymous, Gallery of the Ices of the Château de Versailles, 1678.**

This masterpiece was begun in 1678, when Versailles became an official residence. After signing the Nimègue peace accord, which was the height of his reign, Louis XVI commissioned Le Brun to depict the good deeds of his government on the gallery ceiling. Many European rulers drew inspiration from this lavish decor.

Baroque

Originating in Italy and then developing in several other Catholic countries, Baroque set itself apart from the classical style and became the symbol of ornamental richness and an often surprising formal liberty.

Often perceived as the decadence of art under the Renaissance, the Baroque style developed between 1630 and 1760. As the Baroque was implacably opposed to classicism, the two styles divided Europe in half, with each as a vernacular metaphor, an idiom intelligible to two different forms of character: one embodied order, rules, and balance, while the other symbolized whimsy distortion, asymmetry, and abundance. Classicism and Baroque nevertheless managed to coexist, and moreover, even to complement one another.

Grandeur, sensuous richness, and drama—all are descriptive of the Baroque style, whose recurrent motif is the shell, with its curves, solid, and hollow areas. Let us risk using a metaphor: if classicism is the land, with its orderliness firmly planted in the soil, the Baroque is the moving sea, whose waves sweep everything away. Moreover, the term, before entering into scholarly use, was derived from the Portuguese word *barrocco,* meaning an imperfectly shaped pearl.

Adam van Vianen, Pitcher with rubies, 1614. Rijksmuseum, Amsterdam.

OPPOSITE: The hermitage of the margravine Wilhelmine Bayreuth, eighteenth century. Paneling and chinoiserie in the Hall of Mirrors, Munich.

FOLLOWING PAGES: Michael Planer, screen with five leaves, 1653. Oil on canvas. Axel Vervoordt collection.

Jean-Claude Chambellan
Duplessis,
chimney arm, c. 1760.
Sèvres porcelain, London.
Victoria and Albert Museum,
London.

BELOW: Drawing for a
plumed bed canopy, 1743.
Watercolor. Bibliothèque
Nationale de France, Paris.

OPPOSITE: Silver and blue
lounge of the Amalienburg
pavilion, 1734, Munich.

*Built in the Nymphenburg
gardens, summer residence of
the grands electeurs from
Bavaria, this hunting pavilion,
a German rococo masterpiece,
was built by Cuvilliés between
1734 and 1739. The excess of
elaborate ornamentation is
multiplied by the mirrors in
the oval room.*

The Baroque style developed in Italy in response to the growing power of northern Europe and the Protestant Reformation, and what can be considered the art of Counter-Reformation—curved, undulating, broken lines; a multicolored palette; sumptuous materials; explosive combinations; firework artifices; and a frivolity representative of the grand opera of courtly life in Europe at the time. In music, Baroque was even more sonorous and shimmering.

An essentially aristocratic art, the Baroque of the seventeenth century wove a strong link between various European countries, including Germany, Austria, Czechoslovakia, Poland, and Russia. It would blossom in an array of monuments, decors, and postures, whose excesses would actually trigger a revival of classicism in the late eighteenth century, with a return to straight lines and a newly catalogued repertoire of styles (supposedly adaptable to all circumstances). In the Baroque period, architecture, painting, sculpture, and all of the decorative arts, from furniture to the smallest object, formed a whole whose parts were inseparable. It created a universe in which the spectator became the central fulcrum, and with him, an entire courtly society bowed under the exalted weight of its own enthusiasm.

Under the influence of Italy since the Renaissance, the France of Mazarin proved to be the only European country that endured the earthquake of Baroque style only through shock waves. Some even argue that France went directly from High Renaissance to rococo, never fully embracing the Baroque. This is undoubtedly due to

the personality of a great king concerned with his own identity; at Versailles, rationalism and a sense of balance—in a word, consistency—allowed two apparently contradictory but ultimately complementary trends to coexist.

In a rare attempt to create a comprehensive art form, the Baroque style was exported via Spanish galleons throughout Latin America; there it underwent remarkable developments and eventually spread all the way to the Orient and to China, an empire whose whims were actually an extension of the Baroque style.

The endless game of pencil on paper, of curves and countercurves, Baroque would eventually result in rocaille, or rococo, in the eighteenth century. One of the most original ornamental phenomena in the history of decorative art, rococo continued into the twentieth century, well after it ceased to be fashionable. Because the style was founded on exaggeration, bourgeois wisdom mistrusted it and allowed its development only through accumulations of curios. Its unbridled whimsy nevertheless provided a new sense of comfort. On Oriental-inspired couches and in generously curved easy chairs, Europe was, for the first time,

comfortably seated: a posture conducive to conversation, even if, by exalting its own decadence, the rococo style sometimes caused the occasional migraine.

The information sent back from China by Jesuit missionaries in the seventeenth century did much to renew the repertoire of forms inherited from the French East India Company, which had been chartered by Louis XIV to exploit trade in the East. Since that time, chinoiserie, or Asian art, had become a powerful and lasting influence, from the extraordinary tales of the voyages of explorer Marco Polo to the influences of Palermo. Every century since has had its share of exotic inspirations.

Jean-Baptiste Chevillon, design for the decor of a sitting room, second half of the eighteenth century. Bibliothèque Nationale de France, Paris.

OPPOSITE:
Johann Jakob Schübler, drawing for an office, c. 1730. Engraving, in the fourth edition of J. J. Schübler's works, 1738.

The Century of Enlightenment

A time of balance between rococo and neoclassicism, art in eighteenth century France was a combination that invented a new genteel way of life. This period—a high point for creation and especially decor—remains a reference point.

Louis XIV died in 1715. Exhausted by the twilight of a seventy-two-year reign, France discovered a newfound youth. Versailles, the palace of implacable etiquette, remained closed during the seven years of the Regency period. It was a time for inventing a new style and for Paris to open its salons and alcoves. The various facets of the art of living underwent a marked

Pot-pourri pot in porcelain on a pink background, c. 1760, Sèvres Manufactory. Louvre Museum, Paris.

OPPOSITE: François Boucher, *La Toilette*, 1742. Oil on canvas. Thyssen-Bornemisza collection, Madrid.

Louis Nicolael von Blarenberghe, *The Office of the Duke of Choiseul*, 1757.
Painting on ivory, Blarenberghe miniature on a snuffbox by A. Leferre.

PRECEDING PAGES:
Bernard Picart, *La Galerie d'Hercule*, 1740.
Engraving, Lambert Hotel, Paris.

In opposition to the grandiosity of Versailles under the reign of Louis XV, high society opted for homes of more intimate proportions and a different look with specialized furnishings.

FOLLOWING PAGES:
Gilded wood signs in three shades of gold, Louis XV's bathroom, Château de Versailles.

change: with more relaxed mores, shapes became more rounded. People started to think of "essential commodities," ones that would develop the art of conversation and promote privacy—an entirely new concept.

Peace finally reigned and with it prosperity and trade expanded. All of the right conditions came together for the eighteenth century to become a particularly rich and refined period in art history, including the so-called minor arts.

Married at age 15, Louis XV, who was a conservative, was reluctant to make changes to the grandiose environment devised by his grandfather. At the same time, in the capital, architects, paneled-furniture makers, decorative painters, and decorative art dealers were mapping out the century of Enlightenment. It was perceived as the height of easy living, even as its impending end was heralded.

From that time until the French Revolution, the court would encourage a creativity occurring outside of its sphere of influence. There are two Louis XV styles. The first consists of a rational flowering of the Baroque style that had seized hold of all of Europe. This rocaille style, with its shells, light, and majestic curves, produced environments of great formal richness. The decors that would subsequently become known as Pompadour style were happily cultivated by the king's influencial mistress, the Marquise de Pompadour, the queen in all but name, in her numerous residences. These included the Hôtel d'Évreux in Paris, on the edge of the Tuilerie Gardens, which has since become the Élysée Palace.

Around 1750, a second style arose that set the tone for the following reign. In reaction to the rococo style it broke with busy ornamentation in favor of the straight line, and this owed much, once again, to the Marquise de Pompadour and her circle. This return to ancient Greek style was termed neoclassicism. With the very recent exploration of Herculaneum and Pompeii, the new generation became infatuated with "anticomania." In France, Doric columns, friezes, and warrior motifs gradually replaced the Baroque style, which survived for a surprisingly long time

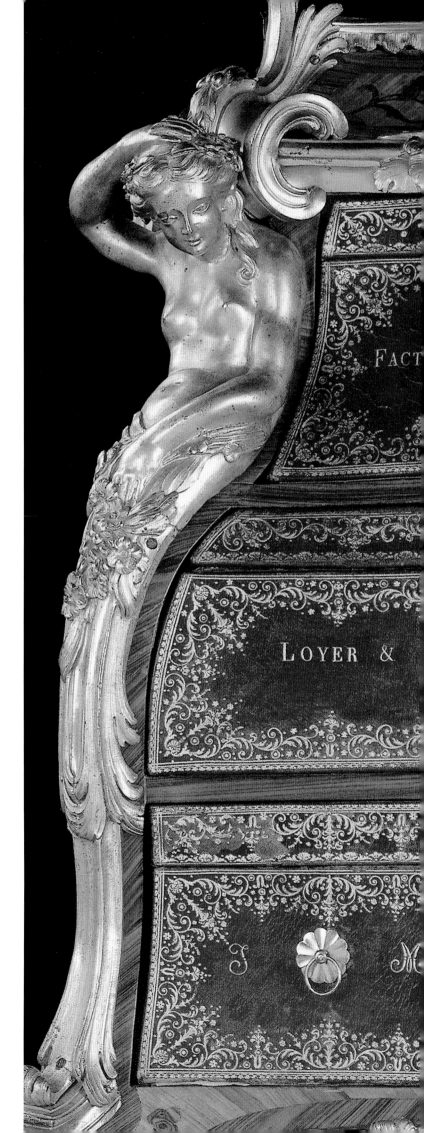

Nicolas Heurtaut,
one of four armchairs, c. 1755.
Wood. Louvre Museum,
Paris.

OPPOSITE:
François Boucher,
*The Marquise
de Pompadour*, 1756.
Alte Pinakothek, Munich.

Harpsichord (signed
Pascal Taskin), 1786.
Victoria and Albert
Museum, London.

OPPOSITE: Delafosse,
bed "à la Polonaise,"
eighteenth-century.
Drawing. Private
collection.

across the Rhine. Across the English Channel, scions of wealthy families were sent to finish their education in Italy; at the same time, they collected antiques whose influence would be felt throughout the nineteenth century in Britain.

If so many subsequent generations have identified with a golden age embodied by eighteenth-century France, it is because, in addition to a relaxing of mores, there was a profound redistribution of living spaces—one that is very similar to our present one. The ancient triad of antechamber, bedchamber, and privy was succeeded by the specialization and diversification of the rooms in a house. Whereas only yesterday, people spent their lives standing in compact groups in a succession of rooms, in strictly codified spaces and postures (when not in bed), during the century of Enlightenment society required a dining room, an adjoining kitchen (these were previously situated far apart), and parlors whose mirrors reflected the brilliance of both the crystals of the chandeliers and the words of their occupants. In powdered wigs and long-trained gowns, like those drawn by French rococo painter Jean-Antoine Watteau, they sat in a circle, exchanging witticisms about suitors or discussing seditious pamphlets. Instead of ceremonial halls, they now preferred small rooms—the boudoir, the dressing room, the library: delightful retreats that were much easier to heat and more conducive to pouring one's heart out. The development of hygiene in the eighteenth century fostered the creation of bathrooms. Louis XV had one installed near his bedchamber at Versailles. Finally, the advent of indoor plumbing allowed for the installation of so-called English style toilets whose flush mechanism was connected to a tank hidden in the ceiling. This must have been quite a relief. But it was particularly the creation of multiple passages and corridors that by preserving intimacy, changed the boundaries between public and private and invented the concept of comfort: homelife was no longer a matter of the soul but one concerned with personal space. For example, a room of one's own was previously unheard of. This was quite a little revolution. In addition to day-to-day architecture, the eighteenth century engendered a diversification of furnishings. These contributed to the attractiveness of the rooms, for which they were often specially designed. This created a feeling of unity and harmony. Here, too, the variety was captivating: secretaries, *bergères* (wing chairs), marquises, settees, commodes (chests of drawers), *bonheurs-du-jour* (fall-front desks)... their very names speak volumes, and they are still the joy of major antique dealers. Many actually find it natural to sit in seats designed for customers half their weight and ten inches shorter! From avenue Foch to Park Avenue, the eighteenth century is not a period, but a state of mind.

The arrival of the dauphine Marie-Antoinette, archduchess of Austria, in May 1770, not only ended the aristocracy's "great style," but also brought about an even more elaborate concept of intimacy. It would no doubt be excessive to assign full responsibility for this evolution to one very young woman. But, in fact, the nobles living at the end of the reign of Louis XV, and the monarch himself, fell in love with the woman whose marriage had been intended for no purpose other than to serve Austrian foreign policy. The king gave her the Petit Trianon as a gift, although it had originally been designed for Madame de Pompadour. Its image of purified classicism, its

FOLLOWING PAGES:
Michel-Barthélemy Olivier, *Musicale at the court of the Prince de Conti, with a Performace by the Young Mozart*, 1766. Oil on canvas. Château de Versailles.

The scene takes place at the time of the debut of an unknown genius in Paris: Mozart, shown here at the harpsichord. In the course of such informal receptions, the most distinguished guests served themselves. At traditional cloth-covered tables, small pieces of furniture on wheels were added, allowing for maximal fluidity and continual arrangement of reception rooms, following the light as it streamed in.

small but perfect proportions, and its exquisite, unornamented composition will forever be associated with Marie-Antoinette, an unfortunate sovereign doomed by her immoderate taste for luxury and her total indifference to cost. With the help of Hubert Robert, Marie-Antoinette created a pastoral hamlet at her Trianon hideaway and had various items designed by her appointed architects/decorators. Breaking with the flamboyant geometric style invented by Le Nôtre, the gardens were of English inspiration. Tall trees, symmetrical openings, and trimmed boxwoods punctuated with classical statuary were abandoned for the studied disorder of a natural setting that was seemingly wild. Thus, the domesticity of the decor echoed the landscape. It was suggestive of a Frenchified Arcadia—the place where, according to legend, people lived in full harmony—where the rustic could coincide with the affected. Courtly French society soon wanted the same finery, the same furnishings, the same decors and regalia as the queen. And that was her undoing. It took place under the

Office of the meridian, for the state of 1781. Versailles museum.

Marie-Antoinette suffered from a lack of intimacy in her quarters where one room led right into another. For the first time in Versailles, this octagonal boudoir, whose doors could be locked, was designed for her.

increasingly critical eye of a people bewildered by such mad consumption, which was nevertheless responsible for the creation of numerous masterpieces. In the private apartments at Versailles, Fontainebleau, Saint Cloud, and other royal residences, white and gold predominated on the paneling, while pastel tones and floral motifs were prevalent for furnishings. The rediscovery of ancient forms resulted in an explosion of tripods, ginger jars, Greek-style vases, fluted pilasters, and Pompeian cherubs, which were popular through the rest of the eighteenth century. It has been said that

this encouragement of solitude fostered a distance between the sovereigns and their subjects. Likewise, by seeking to portray herself as a common woman rather than one with the attributes of royalty, Queen Marie-Antoinette lost her legitimacy. It is a paradox that by striving to be simpler, the powerful distanced themselves from the very target they purported to attract. This ran counter to an age-old tradition of the French monarchy. What remains in the collective imagination is the image of a rebellious beauty: a victim of her own frivolity.

In the heart of Paris, in the Marais, architect Jules Hardouin-Mansart's hotel, renovated by Jacques Garcia in the 1980s.

In this room, the Parisian decorator reconstructed a convincing likeness of the private realm of an honest man at the time of the Enlightenment. A new living arrangement is under way. With a salon, office, waiting room and boudoir, and even a bathroom adjoining the bedroom open only to one's close personal friends. The way private life was organized in the eighteenth century is still how we practice it today. This explains why this era serves as a reference point for those nostalgic for a certain art of living

English Style

Although sensitive to currents of European style, England jealously guarded its independence and invented a decor in the eighteenth century that was entirely its own. Its influence is still seen today across five continents.

"From the time in 1145 when Thomas of London, Saint Thomas of Canterbury, studied canonic law in Auxerre until the more recent period when Walter Sickert studied painting in Dieppe, English culture has been enriched and expanded by constant contact with French thought and erudition," wrote Harold Nicolson in his 1948 preface to the Eight Centuries of British Life exhibition in Paris. Admittedly, England is an island, but it nonetheless thrived on Italian art and French taste. The Victoria and Albert Museum, in London, bears witness to the historical periods when fruitful exchanges nourished the

OPPOSITE: John Zoffany, *The Dutton Family in the Drawing Room of Sherborne Park,* Gloucestershire, collection of the descendants of Sir Peter Samuel, fourth Viscount Bearsted.

English school, Bedroom.
Lithography,
nineteenth century.

In his Strawberry Hill villa, Horace Walpole employed motifs inspired by Westminster Abbey. These are the origins of decor of an archeological character that flourished in England throughout the nineteenth century.

country's decorative arts, reconciling foreign tastes with local customs and needs. In the eighteenth century, during the expansion of its empire, Great Britain acquired a distinct decorative style that would in turn influence the rest of the world. What is generally described as English style, developed between 1750 and 1850, constituted the manifesto of a new art of living.

Considered a golden age even now, the Georgian era, which corresponds roughly with the reign of the first four Hanovers, presided over a simultaneous burgeoning of the country's industrial, maritime, and financial powers. At the same time, democratic ideals slowly took shape. On the whole, the

Continent remained ruled by absolutism, and thus the English monarchs were the first to let the arts and humanities develop on their own. English style in the eighteenth century reveals a remarkable paradox. There were, at least in appearance, two opposing currents, and each was identified by the surname of its main protagonist: Chippendale and Adam. In 1754, the former, cabinetmaker Thomas Chippendale (1718–1779), published *The Gentleman and Cabinet Maker's Director,* a collection of decorative designs that has since become a reference standard. While his work prolonged the effects of the rococo style, it incorporated new exotic elements, a recurrent motif in nations enamored with travel, as England was. In it we find Far Eastern themes mixed with the most flamboyant Gothic styles. Botanical curves interlace with broken-shell motifs, chairs feature lacquered latticework backs, beds include cupolas, pediments are shaped like pagodas, and so forth. But above and beyond, with an eccentricity born out of an annoyance with England's constantly rainy climate, Chippendale was able to combine the fanciful Baroque style with the solid, practical considerations of his fellow Englishmen. In Chippendale's vision, the utilitarian coincided with the luxurious, and the linear facades of the typical brick homes gave no clue to their more turbulent interiors. This duality reveals one of the character traits of the English and is undoubtedly not the least of their charms.

In matters of both dress and furnishings, the English aristocrats wanted essentially to seem like country folk, free to come and go as they pleased. Never in their lives would the concept of pomp and circumstance prevail over considerations of comfort and the remote casualness that is one of the primary privileges of English dandyism.

In 1758, just four years after the publication of Thomas Chippendale's *Director,* a young architect named Robert Adam (1728–1792) returned from Italy. He had gone there, like many of his contemporaries, to ponder the imperial ruins. From his travels, he derived the style that would lend immediate success to his name. Whereas the architecture of the period—designed by the likes of Inigo Jones and William Kent—servilely imitated the ancient style, Adam adapted its principles to the needs of his contemporaries. With a remarkable sense of practicality, he thereby gave the English art of living a more appropriate future, based on elements borrowed from Greece.

Contemporary with Louis XVI, the Adam style pursued the same ends—breaking with grandeur in favor of intimacy—but with different means. It was an early form of

OPPOSITE: Robert Adam, great staircase in the St. Marylebone House, 1773–1776, London.

Thomas Chippendale, chest of drawers in mahogany, manufactured for Rayman Hall, c. 1755.

Sir John Soane's Museum, 1835, London.

Built in the time of George IV, the house museum of Sir John Soane, one of the best architects of nineteenth-century England, remains intact and open to visitors at 13 Lincoln's Inn Fields, London. A true legacy, it simultaneously contains his archives and collection, and furnishings that attests to the modern concepts inspired by the French theoreticians of neoclassicism.

The library, Sir John Soane's Museum, 1835, London.

Conceived in the Georgian era as both a work and a living space, this home devoted to architecture remains one of the most instructive places for its arrangement of space and the effect of one room on another. The light and its reflections was one of Soane's main concerns.

bourgeois Romantic style, with an emphasis on privacy quite close to our own.

Characterized by spaces whose geometry is even, refined, and highly varied, the Adam style features squares, ovals, octagons, and circles—simultaneously. This clarity-infused harmony marries antiquated motifs—often in decoratively painted white gesso—with pastel palettes offset by the sober dark mahogany of the figurative furniture. Nothing was meant to be added or removed from these groupings—other than the artwork that the scions of wealthy families brought back from their Grand Tours of Paris, Florence, Venice, Naples, and Syracuse, where they were greeted by skillful reproductions of local masterpieces. These early souvenirs now constitute a sort of curiosity among collectors.

Like the breeding of thoroughbreds, fox hunting, and the impeccable cut of a frock coat, the Adam style contributed to a ceaseless propagation of the English way of life throughout Europe. This also occurred through the less aristocratic but highly ingenious work of artisans like George Hepplewhite and

OPPOSITE: Etruscan bedroom in Heveningham Hall, designed by James Wyatts, 1790. Suffolk, England.

ABOVE (FROM LEFT TO RIGHT): Robert Adam, ceiling representing the "Adelphi Scheme," 1770. Victoria and Albert Museum, London.

Plates extracted from *Works in Architecture* by Robert Adam, 1773.

Robert Adam, the Kimbolton cabinet: mahogany and oak inlaid with rosewood, slabs of *pietra dura,* and gilded bronze fittings, 1771–1776. Victoria and Albert Museum, London.

FROM LEFT TO RIGHT:
Collection of
architectural plaster casts,
Sir John Soane's Museum,
London.

Design of Soane's dining
room adjoining the library,
London.

Belzoin sarcophagus,
Sir John Soane's Museum,
London.

decorative designers such as Thomas Sheraton. In the 1790s, both men published guides to their furniture collections that prefigured catalog sales. With their highly accurate mass-production techniques, they contributed to disseminating these simple, solid, and comfortable furnishings, which are still considerably in vogue worldwide.

For political reasons, the United Kingdom was the only country to escape the dictatorship of the Empire style. In the early decades of the nineteenth century, England continued to produce its own version of international neoclassicism, known as the Regency style. Its name was inspired by the regency of the

future George IV, but in fact defines a period that extended well beyond his reign (1811–1820). Like his enigmatic personality, the Regency style named for George IV is difficult to pigeonhole. Combining Greco-Roman influences with Chinese exoticism, and antique purity with the art of upholstery, it essentially constitutes the triumph of eclecticism—a new concept greatly influenced by a pronounced taste for travel, which decoratively foreshadows the long reign of Queen Victoria.

In 1850, the British Parliament moved into a solemn, long building in London, inspired by the nearby Westminster Abbey. At the same time, medieval ogees invaded the cottages of the

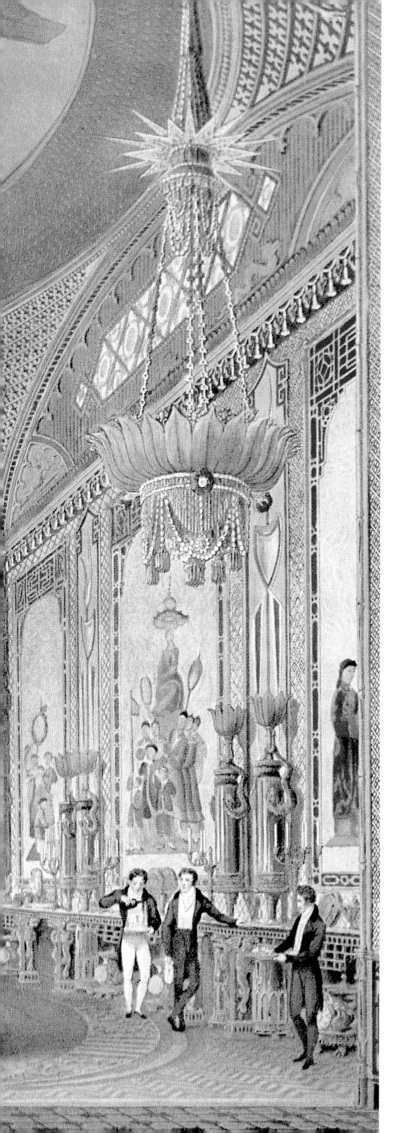

self-made, who were enriched by British trade and industrial progress. In this new society, people prided themselves less on elegance than on well-being. A page of history had been turned. On it, the chaos of the decorative arts would have been written, had not the notion of charm replaced the notion of style—a development that would be fraught with consequences.

John Nash, Banquet hall, Brighton Pavilion, 1822. Leaf from *Views of the Royal Pavilion*, 1826.

Inspired by the Orient, this extravagant room was built by Nash, beginning in 1815, at the request of the Prince-Regent of England, the future George V. It expresses the taste for the exotic, spurred by England's great maritime power. The penchant to cram together a variety of treasures heralded the eclecticism that developed over the course of the nineteenth century under the influence of long-distance voyagers. Hanging from an imaginary sky and partially hidden by the leaves of a banana tree, a silver dragon clasps in his claws the chain of a monumental chandelier with crystal trefoils.

Russian Taste

Under the reign of Catherine II, the decorative arts flourished in Russia. Though this northern empire adhered to Western culture, its own dawn of arts was no less original.

Rare is the ancient city that was planned, built, decorated, and furnished ex nihilo. That was the case with St. Petersburg—a small, marshy port at the mouth of the Neva River, built, at the expense of Moscow, as the capital of all the Russias. For Czar Peter the Great, it was a question of integrating the

Pietro Antonio Rotari, *Catherine II,* eighteenth century. Oil on canvas. Château de Versailles.

OPPOSITE: Interior of the Pavlovsk palace built by Charles Cameron between 1782 and 1786 for Catherine II. The interior decoration was conceived by Maria de Wurtemberg, the wife of Czar Paul I.

ABOVE AND RIGHT: Interior of the Pavlovsk palace.

Built in the Palladian spirit in 1782, the palace of Catherine II owed much to Italian stucco artists from the Lake Como region. Their antique designs, whose coldness is accentuated through the systematic use of white, suffered considerably in the 1941 German invasion. But the pieces that were safeguarded allowed the Soviets to reconstruct them with remarkable authenticity. The furniture was placed in Siberian mine shafts to protect it from bombs.

northern empire into the family of nations. The site, on the Gulf of Finland, constituted one of the only windows to the West. The monarch and the empresses who succeeded him made use of every available talent. But it was the Semiramis of the North, as Catherine II (1762–1796) was nicknamed, whose personality veritably forged the city's identifiable style.

Corresponding with d'Alembert, Voltaire, and Diderot; buying or commissioning masterpieces; enlisting the talents of foreign architects; building palaces; planning plazas, gardens, and avenues; putting together immense collections of all sorts; and fostering the sciences, Catherine appropriated the trends of

her day so well that she created an atmosphere in St. Petersburg that, while admittedly composite, was nevertheless singular in its vision. This cerebral woman had a passionate affair with the architect Charles Cameron (1740–1812), which resulted in many brilliant works. On Cameron's arrival in 1779, she wrote to the Baron von Grimm, a German critic who kept her informed of the latest trends: "At present, I have shanghaied Mr. Cameron, Scottish by birth, a Jacobite by faith, a great designer bred on antiquities and known for his book on the ancient baths. We are fashioning here with him a terraced garden with baths below and an arcade above; this will be beautiful, beautiful...."

Vase in carved and gilded steel, eighteenth century. State Hermitage Museum, St. Petersburg.

In times of peace, the arms manufacturers of Tula created furniture and steel objects of a very rare quality, cut by diamond point for Catherine the Great. Generally, these were given as imperial gifts.

OPPOSITE: **Office, 1782–1786. Pavlovsk palace, Pavlovsk, Russia.**

Thus, both the delicate Adam style and motifs from Pompeii entered the imposing imperial residences of Russia. At the same time, the German cabinetmaker David Roentgen (1743–1807) designed their furnishings, admittedly inspired by Parisian creations, but with a militant luxury and sober richness that sparked a flurry of Russian production for use by the powerful. These generally impressive decors were distinguished by the use of precious materials such as malachite, jasper, lapis lazuli, and agate. In 1765, Catherine sent an expedition to the Urals to take inventory of the resources there. She also engaged the Tula arms-works to produce valuable steel furnishings cut with a diamond stylus and decorated with ormolu.

The Oranienbaum, the sovereign's country residence, also called the Personal Dacha; the Peterhof and Pavlovsk palaces, the properties of Catherine's son; Czar Paul I, and other residences built in the desolate environs of Petersburg all bear witness to this distinct Russian style, despite the depredations of war. These structures reflect a mixture, where military gear coincides with the charm of trompe l'oeil, and luxurious frivolity with quasi-rustic mores. After taming Western influence, all the better to break free of it, this style endured, with varying degrees of success, until the fall of the empire and beyond.

FOLLOWING PAGES: **Dining room, 1782–1786. Pavlovsk palace, Pavlovsk, Russia.**

Gustavian Style

Many sovereigns attach their own names and styles to an era. As for the seductive Gustav III of Sweden, he engendered a neologism that came to define the spare and charming eighteenth century illuminated by the cold light of the North.

Far from Rome and Paris, up in the North flourished an original style influenced by European neoclassicism. In 1771, at the age of 23, Prince Gustav of Sweden regretfully abandoned the pleasures of the court of his friend King Louis XVI and mounted his own throne, creating a role for Swedish society on

Lorenz Pasch the Younger, *Gustav III, King of Sweden,* 1771. Oil on canvas. Sholb Ambras collection, Innsbruck.

Gustav III wearing the official costume he designed for the gentlemen of his court.

OPPOSITE: Dining room in the Regnaholm house, Sweden.

the chessboard of the great powers. As is often the case, his determination was accompanied by the active encouragement of the fine arts. The "Gustavian style" was born of a certain dearth of resources coupled with the monarch's passion for architecture. Elegance, charm, and a love for all things French—tinged with a degree of coldness—blended with personal comfort in Scandinavian interiors. Voltaire, Linnaeus, Rousseau, and Beaumarchais expressed their admiration for this distant kingdom that has demonstrated such remarkable creativity. In Swedish castles, time seems to stand still. This is a country that has never known war, revolution, or architects with ulterior motives. Many complexes remain intact, preserved by the crystalline ice of Sweden's beautiful and melancholy light that illuminates without heating.

In 1810, the arrival in Sweden of Bernadotte from France—the founder of the current dynasty—reinforced the links between the two countries' styles. In Sweden, this reflected a simplicity that made the Gustavian style seem almost modern. Thus, around 1990, a century exhausted from so much upheaval rediscovered the charm of a Sweden that had been forgotten in a cor-

ner of the eighteenth century. The infatuation with this revival led the very popular furniture chain Ikea—a Swedish company—to popularize a Gustavian line, which showcases common sense, functionality, graceful simplicity, and the refined lines of plain wooden furniture in lacquered, ivory, or vividly colored finishes. The intimate connotations of the originals rendered their imitations entirely credible. One would think the Gustavian style was a late twentieth-century invention.

Pehr Hilleström,
The Oldest, 1779. Oil on canvas, Drottningholm.

OPPOSITE: Tompette wine vase, engraved with the king's monogram, c. 1770. Sweden.

FOLLOWING PAGES: Rooms of the Regnaholm house (actual state).

The private life of nobles in the royal castle: the family surrounds King Gustav,
who consults the plans for future arrangements. Meanwhile, a gentleman reads aloud.
The gauze curtains have the same assorted designs as the taffeta wall coverings.

Monticello

One of the most remarkable men in politics, Thomas Jefferson was also a humanist and man of all the arts. For his home in Virginia, he designed an environment marked with classicism, good sense, and elegant sobriety.

The third president of the United States of America, from 1801 to 1809, Thomas Jefferson personally drew the plans for his home in Monticello, Virginia, as well as designed most of its decor, furnishings, and the remarkably functional objects with which he surrounded himself. With an enlightened mind, he brought to the art of governing an art of living that still sets the standard for patrician America. Born in 1743, Jefferson was a writer, politician, lawyer, scholar, and, in a word, a truly honest man. At the age of 33, Jefferson penned the young republic's Declaration of Independence.

Thomas Sully,
Portrait of Thomas Jefferson, 1856, Monticello, Virginia.

Jefferson Vail, *Monticello*, c. 1820.
Watercolor, Musée national de la Coopération
franco-américaine, Blérancourt.

Before taking office as president, Jefferson was the ambassador to France during the initial rumblings of the French Revolution between 1784 and 1789. With his intellect and his triumphant taste for the antique, the young leader of the American Enlightenment forged his own style in the Federal period of American design. Jefferson's global vision would spur him to spend forty years designing, using Monticello, his Virginia estate, as a test tube. At Monticello, the influences of Palladio and Rousseau cohabited alongside the aesthetic of the salons of old Europe and the masculine simplicity of a rational mind. The president designed his office furniture, laid out his gardens, and regimented his world by inventing a restrained luxury for which Monticello is still an object of pilgrimage.

Moreover, very early on, Jefferson heralded a modern sensibility—that of functional beauty. The sole case of a president/designer in America, Jefferson would set an example for a number of American First Ladies, who in turn, would impart their own styles on the White House. The most notable was Jacqueline Kennedy; the popularity of what she accomplished was undoubtedly derived in part from a sense of continuity.

OPPOSITE AND ABOVE:
Views of Monticello.

Influenced by Palladio in architecture, and by French neoclassicism in furniture, Jefferson, then secretary of state, acquired beginning in 1790, a collection of furniture that he accommodated for his own use with the greatest care. The collection earned him as much criticism as some of his reforms.

Auguste Garneray, *Josephine's Music Room*,
Watercolor. Châteaux de Malmaison et Bois Préau, c. 1812.

Empire

Inseparable from the autocratic personality of Napoleon I, this style developed apace with his ambitious plans. Breaking with the previous regime, the new state power sought its legitimacy through a return to antiquity.

Like Louis XIV when he took power, from the inception of his reign, Napoleon Bonaparte (1769–1821) understood that the style he set would be essential to his legitimization. But

while the former was part of a continuity—the Bourbon line—Napoleon's regime broke with the past and invented a new repertoire of forms, a new symbolism, and new mythologies. This was precisely the ancient revival that had been occurring since the latter half of the eighteenth century that incited him to turn to Athens and Rome, which were also the

Jean-Auguste-Dominique Ingres, *Bonaparte as First Consul,* 1804. Oil on canvas. Musée d'Armes, Liège.

Jean-Baptiste Isabey,
*The Emperor Napoleon
in his study at the Tuileries,*
c. 1806. Musée d'Anvers,
Belgium.

OPPOSITE: Library of the
emperor in Malmaison.

*Doric columns divide the study
and support a ceiling and arches
decorated with profiles of writers
from antiquity and their names
or works. A pergola motif decorates
the vault above the door, which
opens to the Empress Josephine's
park. Percier and Fontaine
designed the room, with a desk
in light mahogany.*

cradles of two republics that had served as referents for the spirit of
the Revolution. Archeology was a science still in its enthusiastic infancy throughout Europe, and the excavations at the Herculaneum,
Pompeii, and Etruscan sites were sources of inspiration. The archeological findings furthered knowledge of Greek classical designs. The
geometric division of panels and polychrome walls reinforced by the
restraint of mahogany furnishings, thin columns that supported ceilings patterned with striped tents or celestial clouds dotted with
doves, and tones inspired by Greek kraters and arabesques discovered amongst the ruins were some of the stylistic influences, as were
palmettos, Grecian friezes, ova, and rows of pearls. Each detail
reconstituted an ancient world that seemed to foretell a new day. But
like everything that involved Napoleon, haste governed the development of the style that bears not his name, but the broader title of
Empire, taken from his self-proclaimed status as emperor. Painter
Jacques-Louis David (1748–1825), archeologist Quatremere de

Quincy (1755–1849), and architects Charles Percier (1764–1838) and Pierre-Francois-Leonard Fontaine (1762–1853) were part of a small but active group who took part in the great adventure of their Corsican contemporary, and strove to level the past so that a new generation of centurions might use their furniture.

Satyrs and bacchanals, S-scrolls and lion paws, sabers and fasces lictoriae (bundles of sticks that were an ancient Roman symbol of power, but that came to symbolize Napoleon), laurels and vines all gave Parisian salons the look of army camps, where a desire for victory was the ultimate motivation. Another military inspiration, tenting, achieved by draping fabrics on walls or around beds to trigger up the look of a battlefield interior. From the omnipresence of gold initial *N*s to the overt display of trophies of war, the Empire style was a question of depicting each and every detail of the irresistible progression of the eagle's flight. From this perspective, the Egyptomania that seized France, while its armies were experiencing tragic difficulties at the base of the pyramids, is a good example of image manipulation and the powers of decorative art. The banks of the Nile had long been

OPPOSITE: Music room, Hôtel de Beauharnais, current residence of the German ambassador, Paris.

ABOVE: (LEFT CENTER AND RIGHT) Empress Joséphine's bedroom in the Château de Malmaison.

Bedroom, Hotel de Beauharnais, Paris.

Jacques-Louis David,
Madame Récamier, 1800.
Oil on canvas. Louvre
Museum, Paris.

The chaise longue in mahogany,
designed by Jacob, is today part of
the collection at the Louvre.

the image of both the cradle of civilization and the forbidden fruit. By embarking for that distant world in May 1798, Bonaparte did more than just rekindle its attraction. He launched a remarkable self-promotion campaign, which doubled as a scientific expedition. The team of 165 scholars led by diplomat and administrator Dominique-Vivant Denon (1747–1825) brought back the reports, studies, and drawings that would constitute Denon's multivolume *Travels in Upper and Lower Egypt During the Campaigns of General Bonaparte.* Published in 1802 along with hundreds of engravings, the work would have an enormous influence on his contemporaries and on ornamentation. In effect, a military fiasco became a cultural victory. Thereafter, furnishings with sphinx heads, and pyramid and obelisk motifs sprouted up in interiors, constituting one of the early forms of preromantic exoticism.

Denon would become the general director of the Napoleon Museum, which eventually became the Louvre, holding numerous foreign works taken from the plunder of the Grand Army.

It was essentially the ancient style interpretations of Napoleon's personal decorators Percier and Fontaine in their *Recueil de décorations intérieures* (1802–1812), a series of albums of furniture and interiors, that contributed to solidifying the new emperor's official style. Also of influence was Georges Jacob (1739–1814), a cabinet-maker known for his carved wood chair designs during the reign of Louis XIV, in the Waterloo campaign, and beyond (his sons continued the legacy). Napoleon's reign also expanded the artisan industries, including the weaving of cotton calico and Lyon silk. In response to the orders of their monarch and a new courtly lifestyle, the cream of imperial society saw it as a duty to maintain a level of

Ambroise-Louis Garneray, *Queen Hortense in her boudoir*, 1811. Watercolor. Paris.

Napoleon I's beautiful daughter-in-law is represented in the intimacy of her home in the road of Antin, the fashionable district at the time. Queen Hortense is shown in the intimacy of her hunting home in d'Antin—then the fashionable neighborhood. Triangular scalloped garlands, reflecting a neo-medieval taste, hang from the cadet blue ceiling Napoleon III later placed the two jewelry cases dating from the royal family collection in the imperial quarters of Château de Saint-Cloud.

luxury where discernment oftentimes yielded to conspicuous consumption. A paradox of military absolutism, the reasons for which are obscure, the sober masculine lines and shapes of the Empire style were matched with an often tawdry pomp, sometimes causing it to be described as nouveau riche. The grandiloquence of these decors, like the noble titles of those who commissioned them, did not completely founder with the collapse of the Napoleonic regime.

With its decor intact, as well as part of its gardens, the Château de Malmaison, bordering the Seine west of Paris, features the decor most evocative of the charms of life in the days of Consul Bonaparte and his wife Joséphine de Beauharnais, who purchased the palace, redecorated it, and acquired it after their divorce: light fashions and morals to match.

With the dawn of the nineteenth century, the Empire inaugurated a radically new era, one with the promise of a bright future: the era of design. Until then, the various construction trades, decorators, trend-setters, and designers worked individually, and their creations were brought together by a patron. With the Empire—as it was important to establish a clearly identifiable style ex nihilo for political reasons—architects, designers, and artisans all worked as part of the same movement, as if with a single hand, whether the object was a pediment, a place setting, or the curve of a chair. Therefore, for the first time there was a consistency and a reproducibility that could be considered a style. Its reality was all the more tangible in the already large administration needed to run a vast empire, with its many branches requiring equipment, furnishings, and capital goods justified by and exemplary of the new state's prestige. With these mass-produced goods, we enter a completely new phase of furnishing history. Now, in addition to their amusements, nineteenth century officials actually had to take care of business.

Biedermeier

Originating in Austria and Germany with the return of peace in 1815, this style—its furniture and decoration—is distinguished by a simplicity, functionality, and modesty that led it to be dismissed for a long time.

A revival of the charms of domesticity after a period of splendor and battles in Austria, Germany, and a good part of Europe, the Biedermeier style reflected a reaction to Napoleonic imperialism. Long neglected and deemed petty bourgeois, although these are precisely the characteristics that constitute its charm, between 1815 and 1850 this style nevertheless displayed an authentic richness and noteworthy sense of invention. While they fall within the neoclassical repertoire, Biedermeier paintings, decors, and various furnishings are the products of regional artisanry and stand out due to their

Console in cherry wood and ebony. Private collection, Vienna.

OPPOSITE: Julius Oldbach's geneological tree, 1828. Kunsthalle, Hamburg.

Desk chair in ebony-style blackened pear wood. Private collection, Austria.

TOP: Franz Xaver Nachtmann, *Bedroom of Princess Elizabeth of Bavaria*, c. 1840. Watercolor. Sans Soucis, Potsdam.

remarkable simplicity: pure lines, fruit woods enhanced with darker inlays, a lack of ornamental bronze work, etc. The late nineteenth century and the Art Deco period, from Hoffmann to Ruhlmann, would hark back to that functional moderation, which was completely innovative in its day. Likewise, in the late twentieth century, along with the Viennese Secession style, people would rediscover this classical revival that bore the seeds of modernity.

In Vienna in 1822, there were some 950 workshops, most working in the Biedermeier style. Contrary to popular opinion, Biedermeier does not take its name from a cabinetmaker, but rather was a nickname. A humorous combination of the adjective *bieder* (simple, unpretentious) and *Meier* (the most common German last name), *Biedermeier* implies a conventional everyman. But despite its

denotation, the Biedermeier style is stamped with refinement and, situated between Empire and Regency, is easily distinguishable—although, after 1830, like many other styles it was much copied and thereby diminished in value.

Marked by the rise of a new social class of well-to-do merchants, the Biedermeier era promoted domesticity, with its leisure arts, during the peaceful period that followed the Congress of Vienna. In Europe, literature and the arts blossomed during these years, including Goethe's *The Sorrows of Young Werther*, the quartets of Schubert, the art of needlepoint, diary writing, and evening prayers. Airy, flowery, barren, almost poor, the atmosphere during the Biedermeier years exuded sweetness and was tinged with an unspeakable melancholy that is often the mark of uneventful periods.

Clock in mahogany, birch and burr maple. Private collection.

TOP: Eugen Napoleon Neureuther, *Queen Theresa's Bathroom in Tegernsee Castle*, 1840. Watercolor. Sans Soucis, Potsdam.

Romantic Style

It's bright, light, and feminine, but also historical. Nineteenth-century literature describes it abundantly: a decor that accompanied the rise of the bourgeoisie. Pleasant and pretentious, many of these Romantic furnishings are still with us today.

Disdain for the nineteenth century cast a shadow over the period of the Restoration—the reign of Louis XVIII (1814–1824) and Charles X (1824–1830), which each lasted fewer than ten years. This era preceded the reign of Louis-Philippe I (1830–1848, a period known as the July Monarchy). He was the son of Louis-Philippe Joseph, duke of Orleans. The latter had voted for the death of his cousin Louis XVI; this regicide separated him from the Legitimist nobles and drew him closer

Room decorated by Madeleine Castaing in the Château de Lèves, close to Chartres, c. 1930.

to democratic England. This event actually had a great impact on the decor of the period. Having depleted neoclassical sources, architecture and interior decoration turned to retrospective styles, better known as revivals. One of these was the Gothic style, rediscovered thanks to the founding in 1796 of the Museum of French Monuments by Alexandre Lenoir (1761–1839).

The nostalgic evocation of the Middle Ages, with its troubadours and religious ambiguities, was part of the Gothic revival that a few erudite English aristocrats brought to France, which was emerging from numerous political upheavals at the end of the

With disparate elements found while looking for antiques from the interwar years, one of the great decorators of the 1950s re-created a contemporary atmosphere of the heroines Lamartine and Vigny.

eighteenth century. Some ninety years later, France would turn to fanciful historicism, leading to the reconstruction of the castles of the Loire Valley, as well as new designs for everyday items such as dressing tables and streetlights. The boudoir became a chapel, the garden a cloister, with chairs suggestive of prie-dieu and turrets appearing in the corners of the most humble abodes. Another contributor to the revival of the architecture of the Middle Ages was the political leader and writer Chateaubriand, who published his magnum opus, *The Genius of Christianity,* in 1802.

At the same time, large factories were developed; industry took shape, and with it, the notion of decorative art. Soon the first World's Fairs and the rise of consumer middle classes brought about a golden age of mass production, dominated by a Romanticism that sent it in all directions. Alfred de Musset wrote in 1836, "Our century is shapeless. We have imprinted the style of our time neither on our houses, nor our gardens, nor on anything else. From every century, save our own, we have things that had never been seen in any other period." The era's penchant for stylistic imitation nevertheless engendered high-quality products that, in retrospect, bear witness to an originality that was often unintentional yet always quaint. Furthermore, technology now made it possible to mechanically produce large numbers of parts that had previously required many hours of skilled labor. For example, wallpaper replaced loftier materials, offering veritable panoramic decors. At the same time, the techniques of electrotyping and casting caused the spread of a nineteenth-century bourgeois epidemic: the knickknack. Bronze, crystal, ceramics, pieces of silverware, and goldwork: it was the zenith of crafts that would become the glory of Paris and the French arts. Art and industry became inseparable. A few people of insight, alarmed by such disarray, soon attempted to curb this excessive production by calling for a return to classical forms. Thus, in the latter half of the nineteenth century, the Union of the Decorative Arts was founded to provide the creators of what was not yet termed "design" with repertoires of forms. As beauty combined with utility and form endeavored to follow function, a far-reaching debate was in the making.

The fact remains that the Romantic era—a relatively peaceful period throughout Europe—was above all one of rediscovered

femininity. Swordsmen gave way to duchesses presiding over salons, and to the Madame Bovarys, moping amid their light opaline woods, floral wreaths, and needlepoint tapestries. Jardinieres and worktables abounded in the essentially democratic first half of the Restoration. Under Louis-Philippe, with the rise of the bourgeoisie and its watch-fobbed pharmacists, the style became more austere and sanctimonious, and rococo was likened to a form of debauchery.

Noble blood, bureaucrats, the petty bourgeoisie, the working class: the fabric of society was being woven, and its respective decors scarcely varied for a hundred years. The best history of the century's decoration was written in *The Human Comedy*. In the wake of Balzac, Victor Hugo, Gustave Flaubert, and Madame de Girardin, who would write at length about lifestyle with reams of pictorial materials; one could say decorating magazines were born right then and there.

S. Meevrouw, *Interior of the house of Dr. Vrolik,* 1837. Watercolor. Van Hoogenhuize-Gevers collection, Hilversum.

Despite the stiffness of the striped floor and furniture pushed against the walls, Dutch interiors exude a certain gentleness of their own. Music was the primary pastime. Here, the young ladies of the house practice a four-hand piano piece.

A prolific poet, dramatist, and novelist, Victor Hugo was in all things a man of commitment. A royalist in his youth, a Bonapartist later, and then an ardent Republican, he was elected to the French Parliament in 1848. Following the *coup d'état* in which Prince Louis Napoleon overthrew the Republic on December 2, 1851, the polemist was banished from France. He went to live on the Anglo-Norman island of Guernsey, within sight of the French coast. From this tempest-battered rock, the illustrious partisan of a liberal and humanitarian democracy never ceased apostrophizing the man who became Napoleon III—who actually owes his poor reputation, in large part, to Hugo.

Many writers devote a good deal of space in their works to the "spirit" of a place. Victor Hugo was an unusual one insofar as he willingly created surroundings that reflected only his imagination. A Protean genius—we know his talent as a designer—the boredom of exile was undoubtedly one of the reasons for his inspired handiwork.

Although he never stopped writing during the twenty years of his voluntary captivity, the poet also spent a good deal of time decorating his residence, Hauteville House, which was originally built for an English privateer. That modest but luxurious environment is illustrative of the need for escapism: a collision of Oriental fantasy, esoteric symbols, a longing for France, and the need to forget. Not an inch of the house escaped an overornamentation unnerved by its own limitations. "The art of this time should no longer seek only the Beautiful, but the Good as well," wrote Hugo from his rock. The house, which remains intact, reflects neither of those things, but it does at least reflect that perfectly complementary quality: fantasy.

OPPOSITE AND FOLLOWING PAGES:
Hauteville House.
Series of rooms decorated by Victor Hugo during his exile in the port of Saint-Pierre, on the island of Guernsey. Oak gallery in the room, said to be Garibaldi's (OPPOSITE), porcelaine gallery (FOLLOWING PAGES, LEFT), dining room (FOLLOWING PAGES, RIGHT).

The Imperial Feast

A long period of prosperity allowed French society, which was the embodiment of Napoleon III and Empress Eugénie, to bloom. Long held in contempt as a symbol of outlandish wealth, this era has since become a touchstone for decorators.

The artistic haze that surrounded the Second Empire was also integral to it. These nineteen years were the last years of absolute power in France. Everything—and its opposite—has been said about this period.

Napoleon III was never one to inspire unanimity. Nor did the decor during his reign

Franz Xaver Winterhalter, *The Empress Eugénie,* 1854. Oil on canvas. Metropolitan Museum of Art, New York.

OPPOSITE: Sébastien-Charles Giraud, *The Dining Room of Princess Mathilde* (rue de Courcelles, Paris), 1854. Oil on canvas. Musée de Compiègne.

Jean-Baptiste-Fortuné
de Fournier, *Private salon of
Napoleon III at Château de
Saint-Cloud,* 1863.
Watercolor. Fabius ancient
collection.

OPPOSITE: Charles-Raphaël
Maréchal, with the help of
Louis Duveau, the great hall,
apartments of the Duc de
Morny in the Palais du Louvre.

*The paintings represent different
stages of the construction of the
Louvre and of the Tuileries
during the reigns of François I,
Catherine de' Medici, Henri
IV, and Louis XIV. Furniture
in gilded wood with Louis XV
inspiration. In the foreground, a
three-seated chair deemed
"indiscreet," covered in cherry
damask.*

reflect unity. Its identity derives less from the history of style than from technical progress and the remarkable financial boom that brought new social strata to power. The lifestyle of the day would prevail in a worldly and less-than-worldly atmosphere, where comfort, even where stamped by solemnity, became an end in and of itself. Plush draperies and carpets; overstuffed upholstery; an abundance of soft lights; tapestried medallion chairs; love seats and easy chairs grouped around the fireside provided a well-being that was part of a bourgeois continuum, but now took on a symbolic aspect: opulence as morality.

Brought to power by a *coup d'état* on December 2, 1851, Louis Napoleon Bonaparte, the nephew of Napoleon I, restored the empire after a new plebiscite. Dark, pessimistic, and cruel, Bonaparte inspired fear rather than respect. In response to someone who

Fernand Pelez, *A living room in style of the Second Empire*, 1862. Watercolor. Mario Praz collection, Rome.

OPPOSITE: Empress Eugénie's carriage, Compiègne.

The privileged classes were wild about the luxurious silk padding that transformed cars into cozy cocoons and insulated them from the noise of the tracks.

complained that everything was going badly in France, Bonaparte was known for this remark: "How do you expect anything to work in this country? The empress is a Legitimist; Morny is an Orleanist; I myself am a Republican. There is only one Bonapartist and that is Persigny (the minister of the interior). It's insane!"

The same could more or less be said for the rooms in a house during this period of eclecticism. At the time, a drawing room might have been white and gold Louis XV, with seats upholstered in crimson damask, while the dining room was Renaissance-inspired, and the boudoir something straight out of the Petit Trianon.

The emperor was not known for being particularly enamored of the arts. He sincerely believed in progress and was particularly interested in the technical aspects of creativity. He would probably

Eugène Lami, *Staircase in the Entrance to Ferrières Castle,* 1866. Watercolor. Private collection.

Painter and chronicler of the mundane life in the second Empire, Lami (1800–1890) realized a series of interior views of the castle built by the entrepreneur James de Rothschild in Seine-et-Marne in the spirit of the great English country houses.

OPPOSITE: The great dining room in the apartments of the Duc de Morny, c. 1860, in the Louvre. Hunting scenes by Louis-Godefroy Jadin, ceiling by Eugène Appert, and decor sculpted by Émile Knecht.

have been content to live with the interiors designed for his uncle, had he not understood the economic stakes involved in the development of artistic industries and the need to encourage them.

In the 1850s, mechanization, linked to the notion of profitability, began to transform furniture design. The market began to develop, and like its workforce, the upper-class clientele grew by leaps and bounds. At the height of the Second Empire, certain factories in Lyon and the faubourg Saint-Antoine employed as many as five hundred workers. Simultaneously, big cities such as Paris, under the direction of Prefect Hausmann, were restructuring and subdividing, and majestic buildings equipped with modern amenities were sprouting up.

But above and beyond the effects of the Industrial Revolution, behaviors were changing. While people had once ordered furniture

Bénédict Masson,
*Bedroom of the Empress
Eugenie in the Château
de Saint-Cloud,* 1855.
Watercolor. Private collection.

and ornaments directly from the upholsterer or cabinetmaker, in the latter half of the nineteenth century it became common practice, which we follow to this day, to acquire finished products from an intermediary, in which transaction the customer, rarely sure of his own taste, played no part. The price of such mass-produced furniture was consequently lower, but its duration was shorter. Other than in the poorer classes, people would no longer keep their furniture for a lifetime. These practices, which are the basis for fashion as we know it, began to apply to clothing as well. Designer fashion shows, the advent of practical mass production, and seasonal trends similarly dictate our appearance, although over shorter time cycles. But while the fashion designer displays a degree of creativity, the decorator is limited to imitation or perhaps reinterpretation, as

fanciful as it is cold, of the great periods of the past. However, this single source of inspiration would become a pretext for rediscovering certain skilled techniques that the uniformity of the Empire style, followed by the breathlessness of the Louis-Philippe style, had threatened with extinction. From that perspective, throughout this citizens' empire, the extraordinary boom in the furnishing arts, the birth of decorating as we know it, the frenzy of luxury, and the desire to collect or accumulate helped pave the way for the decorative arts in the century to come. Most notably, through mastery of both the industrial tools and the traditional techniques that would be used in what is rightly called, in contrast with the Second Empire, Art Nouveau.

Jean-Baptiste-Fortuné de Fournier, *Salon of the Empress Eugénie in Saint-Cloud*, 1863. Watercolor. Fabius ancient collection, Paris.

With mixed elements from the eighteenth century and modern centuries, this decoration is an example of the reigning eclecticism during the Second Empire. In the center of the room sits the famous desk by Œben and Riesner for Louis XV's office in Versailles.

Arts and Crafts

In the midst of the nineteenth century, just as decor became stuck in pastiche, a group of English prophets advocated a return to the Middle Ages and the lessons of nature, laying the basis for the modern movement that developed over the next century.

In Victorian England, the Arts and Crafts movement represented a form of rebellion against the Industrial Revolution. Although its signature ornamental, decorative excess does not always give an inkling of this, the movement's pioneers believed in the equality of all the arts and were impelled by an objective

Arts and Crafts chair, c.1890.
Sotheby's Picture Library.

OPPOSITE: Morris, Marshall, Faulkner & Co., *The Green Dining Room*, 1865–1867.
Victoria and Albert Museum, London.
Frieze and decoration on plaster by Philip Webb.

Arthur Heygate Mackmurdo, chair in leather and mahogany, c. 1883. Victoria and Albert Museum, London.

OPPOSITE: William Morris, design in watercolor for Jasmine-painted paper, 1872.

that, at the time, seemed nothing less than obvious—"to create beauty in everyday objects." It was an objective that set the course for contemporary design, combating the legitimate concern aroused by production that was as excessive as it was chaotic, and the *bric-à-brac* that every industry generates when left to itself.

In the latter half of the nineteenth century, architecture and the decorative arts were bogged down in stylistic imitation and repetition. The Industrial Revolution brought with it urbanization, and cities became larger. A new bourgeoisie, proud of its status, settled into its furnishings. All the while, smokestacks on the horizon of green alleys revealed the factories where the newly employed populations lived, often in deplorable conditions.

Poet, pamphleteer, designer, reformer, complex character, former architecture student, and jack of all trades William Morris (1834–1896) was the sort of figure who thought of himself as a Jean-Jacques Rousseau. He believed nature was the essential source of all inspiration and that art should exist through and, especially, for the people. In other words, Morris espoused the very opposite of what was represented by the great international exhibitions of art and industry, like those in London in 1851 and Paris in 1855. "In the Middle Ages, everything people produced seemed beautiful, to varying degrees. However, today, nearly all objects produced by civilized people are pathetically ugly and pretentious," condemned Morris,

naively yearning for an infancy of style where an artist was scarcely more than a humble artisan. Hence, Morris was known for his own definition of artistic creation as "man's expression of his pleasure in work." But in blaming the industrialists, Morris neglected to take into account that mass production at the very least had the potential to improve the lives of ordinary people, and that the objects hand-crafted by his own friends—pottery, textiles, wallpaper, etc.—were necessarily unique and, in the end, expensive enough to inhibit production. But above all, Morris's goal was to involve the young visual artists of his day in the nonacademic production of everyday objects. His friends the Pre-Raphaelite painters—Edward Burne-Jones, Dante Gabriel Rossetti, Ford Madox Brown—all belonged to the movement.

FOLLOWING PAGES:
(LEFT) Dante Gabriel Rossetti, *Glorious Gwendolen's Golden Hair,* painting on a chair designed by William Morris, 1856–1857. Delaware Art Museum, Wilmington.

(RIGHT) Sir John Everett Millais, *Lorenzo and Isabella,* 1849. Oil on canvas. The Makins Collection.

Their art itself was bathed in a romantic, dreamlike atmosphere that gave their brotherhood the certainty that it was inventing a new art. In fact, Morris and Co. (Morris finally opened shop) exerted a decisive influence on the relationship between arts and crafts. In a recurrent paradox, what might have appeared to be regressive in fact proved to be a step back in order to make a big leap forward. Faithful to its

principles, in the field of architecture the Arts and Crafts movement generated a domestic revival based on a study of vernacular structures, farms, their flexible designs, their integration into the landscape, and well-proportioned, solid forms, which were always linked to function. Here, too, were teachings with a bright promise for the future, this time in an Elizabethan guise.

Reconstitution of an interior created by William Morris, c. 1860. Victoria and Albert Museum, London.

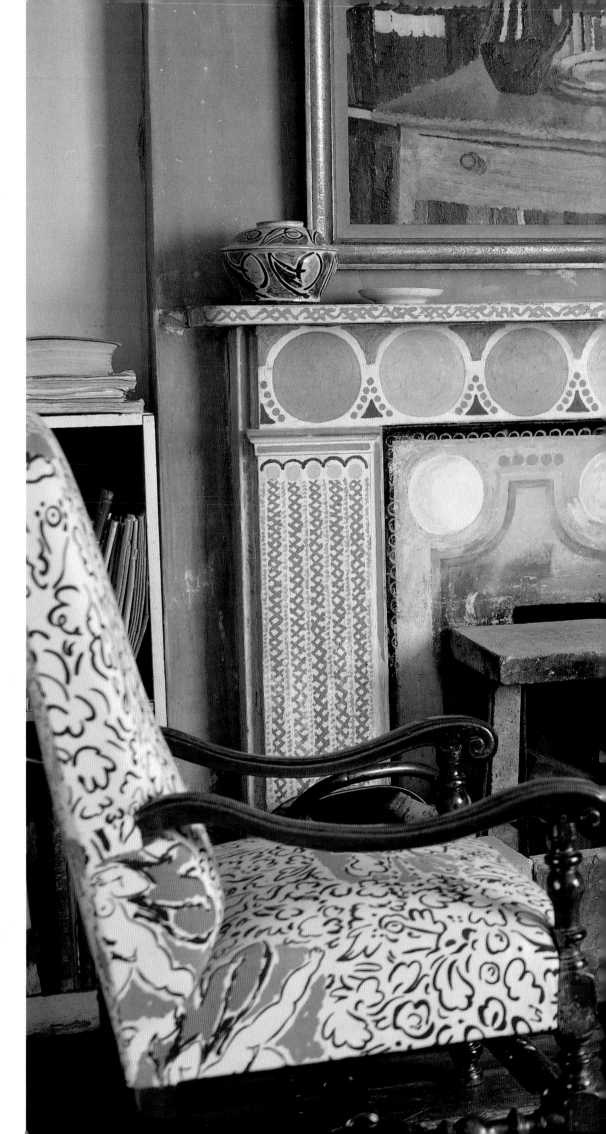

"Bloomsbury"
Clive Bell, office,
c. 1915. Charleston
Museum Trust, England.

*Rectangular chimney
designed by Roger Fry and
constructed in brick and
metal by Bunny Garret.
Armchair covered in a
fabric created by Duncan
Grant and Vanessa Bell.*

Art Nouveau

In 1900, an elite group rose up against academic and pastiche decorators. Their inspiration was plant life. From London to Brussels, from Paris to Vienna, a genuine revolution in the decorative arts bridged revivalism and modernity.

The twentieth century hinges upon those that pre-ceeded it, even if its inventions exceeded those of past millennia. Through diversification, the decorative trends that constitute its milestones came together, overlapped, and even contradicted one another. Several styles emerged on an international scale that would come to characterize the future at the turn of the twentieth century. Mass culture and consumption were its corollaries, speed its vector, and science its guide. As cities became the centers of the modern

Gebruder Thonet, rocking chair, model no. 7500, c. 1880. Vienna.

OPPOSITE AND FOLLOWING PAGES: Victor Horta, interior of Horta's house, 1898–1900. Brussels.

world, nature emerged as a pretext for nostalgia. The upper-middle classes expanded; culture became more accessible and, as a result, advocated new directions. Progress in the visual arts was made by breaking with prior generations. Ornamentation, the very expression of Romantic sentiment, was relegated to trimming for metal frameworks and was infused with aesthetic possibilities resulting from new technologies. Denounced by aesthetes when it was built for the Paris International Exhibition of 1889, the Eiffel Tower became the consummate expression of this pivotal moment, raising the engineer to the level of artist.

Called the Jugendstil in Germany, the Liberty style in London, the Floreale in Naples, and the modern movement in Scotland, Art Nouveau—which took its name from a store in Paris—originated in Belgium and France. It was also derisively nicknamed the "noodle style," due to its whiplash lines, and "metro style," because of the cast-iron entrances designed by Hector Guimard (1867–1942)

for some of Paris's subway stations. The origins of this style, which combines painting and sculpture with the decorative arts in the same building or even the same interior, are complex and full of contrasts. In the 1860s, Eugène Viollet-le-Duc (1814–1879), influenced by his in-depth study of Gothic art, developed a rationalist approach to architecture. This led him to use new construction materials, including cast iron and iron, whose lightness and shapes drew their inspiration from the naves of cathedrals. The architect borrowed his ornamental repertoire from the floral style of the Middle Ages.

In painting, outside of the official circuits where obscurantism—a style characterized by deliberate vagueness—was increasing, the new objective was less to render reality—for that, there was now photography—than to produce a subjective image capable of synthesizing a whole range of sensations. Due to their particularly rich heritage, the French decorative arts combined naturally with this emerging style, with a refinement suggestive of the rococo era. This was particularly the case with work from the School of Nancy—named for a city in northeastern France where artisans such as furniture designer Louis Majorelle (1859–1926) and glassblower Émile Gallé (1846–1904) designed. In Paris, Art Nouveau was characterized by the work of furniture and jewelry designer Eugène Gaillard (1862–1933), sculptor Rupert Carabin (1862–1932), and a host of great decorative designers dominated

by the personality of Hector Guimard, the veritable usher of Art Nouveau to the Parisian landscape.

Elsewhere in Europe, Art Nouveau blossomed. A similar spirit, albeit more sober and architectural, developed in Belgium with the work of architects Victor Horta (1861–1947), Henry van de Velde (1863–1957), and Gustave Serrurier-Bovy (1858–1910), who favored lightness in iron, transparency in glass, and glimmer in ceramics—the Art Nouveau version of American office buildings. In the early 1890s in Scotland, a group of architect-decorators came on the scene and, by transposing the theories of Arts and Crafts, produced a totally original line, embodied by the creations of Charles Rennie Mackintosh (1868–1928).

Georges-Jules-Victor Clairin, *Sarah Bernhardt*, 1876. Oil on canvas. Musée du Petit Palais, Paris.

OPPOSITE: Carlo Bugatti, chair in wood and ivory metal, c. 1900.

Born in 1856, the father of the sculptor Carlo Bugatti and his brother, who would become a famous automobile maker, designed unusual furniture that incorporated parchment, metal, and rare woods.

An architect, furniture designer, and painter, Mackintosh blended the flourish of Art Nouveau with the simplicity of the Japanese aesthetic.

Japan, with its history and art prints, exerted a fascination and provided a fresh artistic influence on Art Nouveau. An Eastern influence can be seen in the famous prints of the British illustrator and artist Aubrey Beardsley (1872–1898), among others.

On the Iberian Peninsula in Barcelona, Antoni Gaudí (1852–1926), developed a highly personal interpretation of Art Nouveau by working with a palette of colorful, broken mosaic tiles, flowing curves, and unusual decorative details. Gaudí's unconventional buildings, octopus-and seaweed-shaped furniture, twisted wrought iron, and rocky concretions offered yet another interpretation of Art Nouveau.

In the United States, Art Nouveau was exemplified by the work of Louis H. Sullivan (1856–1924) and Louis Comfort Tiffany (1848–1933). Credited with building the first skyscraper, the ten-story 1891 Wainwright Building in St. Louis, Sullivan was inspired by Gothic leaf work and naturalistic vines, which were featured in his ornamentation.

Tiffany studied painting, but eventually became recognized for his work in the decorative arts. Focusing on the art of stained glass, the artist created legendary windows and lamps, characterized by their vivid colors and natural forms.

Heralding modernism, while simultaneously embracing ornament, Sullivan prophetically stated: "We must return again to nature and, by listening to its melodious voice, learn like children the accents of its rhythmic cadence." The theater of nature—particularly imposing in the United States—also framed and even defined the new vision with which Frank Lloyd Wright (1867–1959), a student of

Emile Gallé, pâte-de-verre vase, c. 1880. Private collection.

OPPOSITE: Léon Bakst, *The Dinner*, 1902. Oil on canvas. The State Russian Museum, St. Petersburg.

FOLLOWING PAGES: View of the sitting room at the Hill House by Charles Rennie Mackintosh, 1902–1903. Helensburgh, Scotland.

Model of a chair conceived by Charles Rennie Mackintosh for the four tearooms of Kate Cranston, 1900. Glasgow.

OPPOSITE: Charles Rennie Mackintosh, interior view of the Hill House, 1902–1903. Helensburgh, Scotland.

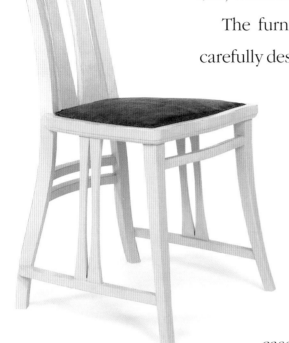

Dining room chair by Peter Behrens, c. 1900.

OPPOSITE: Charles Rennie Mackintosh, the white bedroom, Hill House, 1902–1903.

Sullivan's, imbued his single-family homes in the 1890s. Unrestricted and mostly open to the outdoors via wide decks, which were partially covered by long, flat overhangs, Wright's spaces and complex webs of different volumes and levels remained typically American until 1914, when he presented his work in Europe.

The furnishings of each of Wright's vast rustic houses were carefully designed to fit the spirit of the location and, like the spaces themselves, lyrically reflected an outlook that was both aesthetic and functional, much like the Arts and Crafts movement. Certain models, which have recently been rereleased, show that outside of their specific context they have little relevancy. Like many of the precursors of modernism in the United States, Wright was open about what he owed to the decorative arts of Asia, particularly those of Japan. That was also the case with other West Coast architects and decorators, such as the brothers Charles Summer and Henry Mather Greene, who used local craftsmanship and materials to execute their visions.

Thus, on both sides of the Atlantic, in the last five years of the nineteenth century, each country developed its own domestic variant of this heady aspiration for novelty. The vernacular design as a source of inspiration would last throughout the twentieth century, through thousands of rustic variants. Art Nouveau, per se, reached its peak with the inauguration of the 1900 Paris Universal Exhibition. Replete with optimism, people began to talk about a Belle Epoque.

FOLLOWING PAGES:
Otto Wagner, Schützenhaus: Keiserbad sluice gate, situated on the Danube, 1904–1906. Vienna. The facade was conceived in watertight bricks.

Josef Hoffmann, vase, c. 1900.

OPPOSITE: Gustav Klimt, *Fulfillment*, c. 1905–1909. Watercolor. Galerie Belvedere, Vienna.

Ironically, the Viennese Secession movement reached the pinnacle of its expression in a Brussels hotel designed by Hoffmann for a coal tycoon and decorated with frescos by Klimt.

FOLLOWING PAGES: Dining room of the Stoclet palace, by Josef Hoffmann, 1905–1911. Brussels.

In Austria, alongside Art Nouveau and the Jugendstil, a movement developed that was also inspired by the English Arts and Crafts movement, but that went much further in its exploration of modernity. Explicitly named the Viennese Secession, it brought together artists, architects, and designers who withdrew from exhibitions at the Vienna Academy in 1897 in response to disapproval of their modernist works. Under the leadership of Josef Hoffmann (1870–1956) and Koloman Moser (1868–1918), these progressives formed the Wiener Werkstätte, a guild of craft shops that took a radical approach to furniture, silver, ceramics, and textiles.

A subtle mix of sobriety and refinement with geometric, rectilinear spaces, the Viennese Secession broadly demonstrated that when the stark, straight line emphasized proportional relations, it was as much suited to luxury as to pure functionality. Thus, after a period of decadence, a post–Art Nouveau style was born. In reaction to the mannerism still found in Art Nouveau, this new style mandated remarkable simplicity in an increasingly complex age.

Josef Hoffmann, Seven Ball chair, c. 1906.

ABOVE: Adolf Loos, Villa Karma: view of the dining room, 1903–1906.
RIGHT: Adolf Loos, Villa Karma: entrance hall in marble and gilded mosaic, 1903–1906.

Art Deco

Art Deco designates the first abstract—but not modernist—style of the twentieth century. It influenced decor worldwide, contrasting traditional values with innovation.

In 1908, Picasso painted *Les Demoiselles d'Avignon*, which clothing designer Jacques Doucet later acquired for his studio. The following year, Paris discovered Serge Diaghilev's Ballets Russes, and then, in 1910, Leon Bakst's stage designs for *Scheherazade*, whose primitive and boldly-colored simplicity struck a chord. At the same time, the *Le Figaro* published "The Manifesto of Futurism," by the Italian

Pablo Picasso, *Les Demoiselles d'Avignon*, 1907. Oil on canvas. Ancient collection, J. Doucet, Museum of Modern Art, New York.

OPPOSITE: Jacques Doucet's studio in Neuilly, in 1921. On the wall, *La Charmeuse de Serpents*, by Le Douanier Rousseau. Sofa by Marcel Coard; lacquered table by Eileen Gray.

revolutionary poet Filippo Tommaso Marinetti. On the eve of World War I, Igor Stravinsky's *Rite of Spring* was performed, creating an enormous scandal. This was also the time when Paul Poiret liberated women from the corset, proposing a new, more fluid silhouette of a sensous dancer, freed from Old World customs. The influence of the Orient, Asia, and Africa was seen everywhere: there were new materials, new horizons, and new sensibilities.

For the first time, an era would explicitly take on a comprehensive style, described by a term filled with bright promise: Moderne. This is not to be confused with modernism, which would serve as the nomenclature for the later design movement.

Art Deco can only be thought of in terms of a harmony of different styles, the sum of which were more decorative than functional. The name Art Deco, which was not used by its proponents, came into use well after the 1925 Paris Exposition Internationale des Arts Decoratifs et Industriels Modernes (International Exhibition of Decorative Arts and Modern Industry). Far more than a type of decorative expression, Art Deco reflects a state of mind. It is inseparable from the revolution in the visual arts that took place in the early twentieth century. This was made

OPPOSITE: Pirogue daybed designed by Eileen Gray, rosewood carpentry by Ruhlmann.
Maternity, by Picasso. Collection put together by the Vallois gallery for the Antique Dealers' Biennial in 2000.

ABOVE (FROM LEFT TO RIGHT): Apartment decorated by Paul Ruaud, designer of Eileen Gray's furniture, among them the Serpent and *Bibendum* chairs, 1933.

Eileen Gray, rug conceived for E-1027, c. 1926–1929. Private collection, London.

Eileen Gray and Jean Badovici, sitting room at the E-1027 villa, in Roquebrune, Cap-Martin, 1926–1929.
Bibendum chair; on the floor, *Centimètre* rug, black wool with white design; Transat armchair.

up of many new ingredients: the machine age, abstraction, speed, motion pictures, and, more generally, the vast notion of progress that took hold between the two world wars. An opulent style, as a reaction to the austerity of World War I. Demanding a completely new formal repertoire and framework, its vision could seem at times to be apocalyptic. But after the carnage of World War I, Art Deco assured a definite break with the practices inherited from the Europe of yesteryear, to those who lived through the Roaring Twenties. It would be in America—the New World—now accessible thanks to a revolution in transportation, that everything was being re-invented.

Manhattan, Bombay, Shanghai, and Budapest each created its own version of Art Deco. But it was in Paris that Art Deco was actually invented, circa 1910, as a reaction to the excesses of the declining Art

Jacques-Émile Ruhlmann, interior design for Mme Cernuschi. Black stone, oil pastels, gold paint on tracing paper and vellum, c. 1930.

OPPOSITE: Jacques-Émile Ruhlmann chair, c. 1930.

Gustave Miklos, *Girl,* 1927. Bronze sculpture with transparent black patina.

BELOW: Jean Dunand, spheric vase, c. 1910. Copper encrusted with silver.

Nouveau. While Art Deco's practitioners did not work as a coherent community, Paul Iribe (1883–1935), Paul Follot (1877–1941), Maurice Dufréne (1876–1955), Louis Suê (1875–1968), André Mare (1887–1932), Jacques-Émile Ruhlmann (1879–1933), André Groult (1884–1967), Clément Mère, Pierre Legrain (1889–1929), Eileen Gray (1879–1976), and Jean Dunand (1877–1942) were among the exceptional talents drawn together in France through the decorative arts. They attempted, not without a certain charming hedonism, to reconcile domestic traditions of craftsmanship with a sincere desire to reinvent its forms. Furniture designer Jean-Michel Frank (1895–1941); wrought iron craftsmen Edgar Brandt (1880–1960) and Raymond Subes (1891–1970); goldsmiths and silversmiths Puiforcat (1897–1945) Sandoz, and Goulden; textile designers Raoul Dufy (1877–1953) and Sonia Delaunay (1885–1979): though a diverse group, each adhered to a cohesive design theory in generating geometric, symmetrical, and rectilinear motifs and spaces. These artisans were widely copied in the late 1920s by major furniture manufacturers on the lookout for something new, thus rapidly depreciating Art Deco's value to the elite, due to the lack of originality and poor quality compared with the originals. Throughout the 1930s, the elite either returned to the Classical order or made a radical leap ahead.

Cubist-oriented conventions, however, did continue to expand worldwide until World War II, with a plethora of zigzagging stucco corners, geometric patterns, and stair-stepped motifs. Not to mention the attractive comedy-film sets and ocean liners such as the

OPPOSITE: Jacques-Émile Ruhlmann and Louis Bouquet, minister's room, displayed at the Colonial Exposition in Paris, 1931. This room was reconstructed at the Musée des Colonies de la Porte Dorée, in Paris.

FOLLOWING PAGES: Eugène Printz, André Hubert, and Ivanna Lemaître, Lyautey room, presented at the Colonial Exposition, later reconstructed at the Musée des Colonies in Paris, 1931. Furniture by Printz, with a background of frescos inspired by Asian myths and legends; on the background, a portrait of Marshal Lyautey.

Ile de France and the *Normandie*, which familiarized a broad audience with Art Deco. More strictly speaking, the term Art Deco was coined in Paris in the 1960s to distinguish the progress of French decorative art in 1910–1920 from the Bauhaus movement in Germany and the De Stijl Movement in Holland, and even from the extremist group that gathered around Le Corbusier (1887–1965) and his journal, *L'Esprit Nouveau*. Without relying heavily on the styles that preceded them, the painters, architects, artisans, and interior decorators who formed the Société des Artistes-Décorateurs, or Society of Decorative Artists, aspired to renew their ties with the long tradition of prestige and excellence that had been replaced with stylistic imitation and *bric-à-brac* in the late nineteenth century. Their goal was to change everything so that it would remain the same, without falling into the excesses of an avant-gardism that aimed to make interiors spartan and held that all ornamentation was a crime.

OPPOSITE: Bathroom by Jacques-Émile Ruhlmann, 1937. Ministry of Foreign Affairs (Quai d'Orsay), Paris.

ABOVE (FROM LEFT TO RIGHT): Erté, *Le Choix du Soir*, illustration for *Harper's Bazaar*, March 1923.

The Maharajah's bedroom, by Jacques-Émile Ruhlmann, c. 1930. New Palace, Morvi, India.

Armand-Albert Rateau armchair,
from a set of six, in sculpted oak, created
for Jeanne Lanvin's mansion,
c. 1920–1922.

OPPOSITE:
Armand-Albert Rateau, bathroom
for Jeanne Lanvin's hotel. Reproduced
at the Museum of Decorative Arts in Paris,
c. 1920–1922.

William van Alen, elevator door with metyl wood veneer made by the Tyler Company, 1927. Chrysler Building, New York.

OPPOSITE: Donald Deskey, *Men's Smoking Room,* shown in 1928 at the American Designer's Gallery, New York.

Modernism

Coming up against the craftwork of artist-decorators, between the wars a radical group of European designers strove to create industrial designs that combined beauty and utility, form and function.

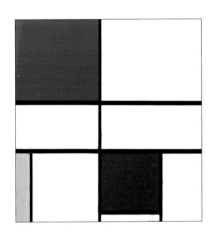

While Art Deco prided itself on the new, it nevertheless continued to subscribe to, rather than challenge, the traditional forms and production methods that preceded it. In contrast, emerging theories advocated that the twentieth century should do away with the past and fundamentally rethink its living philosophy toward the domestic environment, in keeping with the evolution of progressive ideas. One dominant concern that would profoundly transform furniture and product design was how to produce objects of good quality at affordable prices.

While this notion largely escaped Paris's luxury trade, which reveled in its regained prosperity, it was much more relevant across the Rhine. There, the fall of the German Empire caused an upheaval in social conditions and imposed a rigorous and precise reconstruction program through functional architecture. With that in mind, visual artists and architects were called upon to design original forms that directly expressed their function

Piet Mondrian, *Composition C, Composition no. III, Composition with Red and Blue,* 1935. Oil on canvas. Tate Gallery, London.

OPPOSITE: Gerrit Rietveld, interior of the Shröder-Schräder house, by the designer Truus Shröder, c. 1924. Ultrecht, the Netherlands.

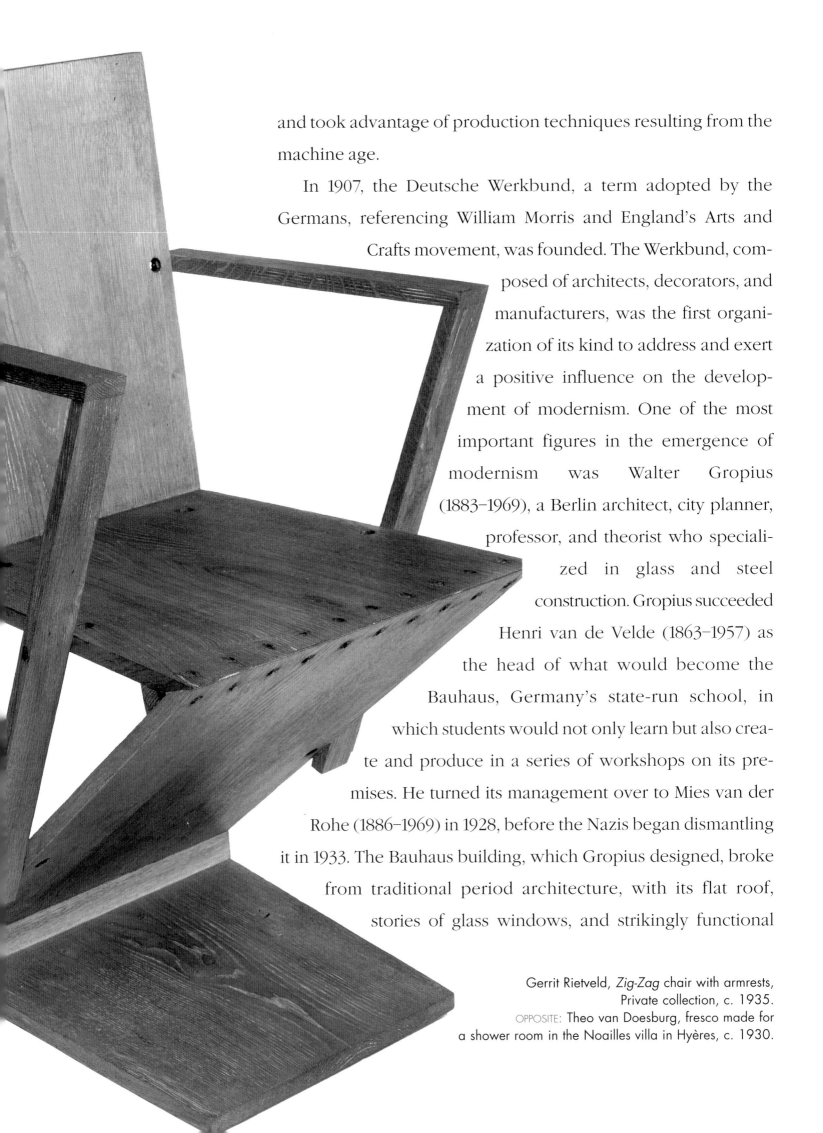

and took advantage of production techniques resulting from the machine age.

In 1907, the Deutsche Werkbund, a term adopted by the Germans, referencing William Morris and England's Arts and Crafts movement, was founded. The Werkbund, composed of architects, decorators, and manufacturers, was the first organization of its kind to address and exert a positive influence on the development of modernism. One of the most important figures in the emergence of modernism was Walter Gropius (1883–1969), a Berlin architect, city planner, professor, and theorist who specialized in glass and steel construction. Gropius succeeded Henri van de Velde (1863–1957) as the head of what would become the Bauhaus, Germany's state-run school, in which students would not only learn but also create and produce in a series of workshops on its premises. He turned its management over to Mies van der Rohe (1886–1969) in 1928, before the Nazis began dismantling it in 1933. The Bauhaus building, which Gropius designed, broke from traditional period architecture, with its flat roof, stories of glass windows, and strikingly functional

Gerrit Rietveld, *Zig-Zag* chair with armrests, Private collection, c. 1935.
OPPOSITE: Theo van Doesburg, fresco made for a shower room in the Noailles villa in Hyères, c. 1930.

Wassily Kandinsky, *Orange*, 1923. Museum of Modern Art, New York.

and ornament-free design that came to exemplify the ideals of the international style.

Gropius attracted a faculty of great artists who would leave their mark on Europe, including Wassily Kandinsky and Paul Klee, two of the most famous, as well as Marcel Breuer, Lyonel Feininger, Hannes Meyer, Oskar Schlemmer, and Laslzo Moholy-Nagy.

Already perceptible in Art Deco, geometric abstraction dominated the aesthetic pursuits of the avant-gardists. But their new-found formalism was totally unrelated to the order, harmony, and ornamentation of a French tradition adjusted to the tastes of the Roaring Twenties.

Gropius, along with his peers, gave birth to what he called "total architecture," using translucent curtain walls, and concrete on steel

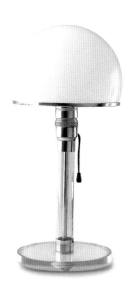

Karl J. Jucker and Wilhelm Wagendfeld, table lamp in glass, 1923–1924.

OPPOSITE: Walter Gropius, Laslzo Moholy-Nagy's dining room in the Bauhaus school of Dessau, 1925–1926.

frame construction building blocks. Like the man himself, total architecture endeavored to master all industrial processes: prefabricated construction, mass-produced furniture, textiles, ceramics, etc. In the 1920s, such constructs considerably influenced the housing units and furnishings produced by the Weimar Republic. But the rise to power of National Socialism, with its retrograde theories, resulted in a wave of emigration by the Bauhaus artists, who generally opposed the regime. Many ended up in the United States—evidence of the shift of the epicenter of design from one side of the Atlantic to the other—and propagated theories of what would become known as the international style on the new continent and then throughout the world.

During this time, a highly ambitious aesthetic movement was developing in Holland. It crystallized around *De Stijl*, a magazine founded in 1917 by painter, designer, and theorist Theo van Doesburg (1883–1931), who published it until his premature death.

Intentionally contemplative and reserved, like the traditional Japanese art that inspired it, neoplasticism, the theory van Doesburg developed with the artist Piet Mondrian (1871–1944) was based on structural rectangularity, the use of pure color, and a total absence of naturalistic decoration. As a result of this particularly radical asceticism, artistry was reduced to pure geometrization, free of any anecdotal connotation or reference to external reality. This quest for fundamental form and absolute purity might have seemed a total negation of art until it became a recurrent theme in the twentieth century: Gerrit Rietveld (1888–1964), J. J. P. Oud, Georges Vantongerloo, and other Dutch artists and architects would follow suit. The design emblematic of this utopian society remains Gerrit Rietveld's *Blue-Red Chair*, which consists of unadorned boards nailed together on a structure of rectangular strips of wood. Originally unpainted, they were subsequently colored red and blue.

Living in Paris in the late 1920s, van Doesburg, too extremist to

FROM LEFT TO RIGHT: Office in the Bauhaus school, with a chair by Walter Gropius, 1920. Bauhaus Archive, Berlin.

Team of designers in Dessau. (FROM LEFT TO RIGHT) Josef Albers, Marcel Breuer, Guntha Stolzl, Oskar Schelmmer, Wassily Kandinsky, Walter Gropius, Herbert Bayer, Lazlo Moholy-Nagy, and Hinnerk Scheper, c. 1927.

Marianne Brandt, tea infuser and strainer, 1928–1932. Silver and ebony.

Fernand Léger,
Charlotte Perriand,
Le Corbusier, Albert and
Pierre Jeanneret, and a
friend at the CIAM
conference, 1923, Athens.
Charlotte Perriand Archives,
Paris.

OPPOSITE AND FOLLOWING PAGES:
Le Corbusier, *L'Esprit
Nouveau* pavilion, 1925.
Reconstructed for *L'Esprit
Nouveau*, le Purisme à Paris,
1918–1925, for the Musée
de Grenoble in 2001.

produce much, was commissioned, through the intervention of the sculptor Robert Arp and his wife, Sophie Taeuber, to rebuild the gigantic café-restaurant-movie-theater l'Aubette, in Strasbourg, France, after it burned. This project remains a reference standard. In 1929, van Doesburg built his own studio house on the hill at Meudon.

De Stijl consisted more of theory than of practice. While the movement was credited for its influence on the Bauhaus, it was essentially Mondrian's revolutionary compositions, which aimed at making visual art explode from its frame, that ensured its posterity.

UNION OF MODERN ARTISTS

Crime and Ornament: It could be the title of a novel about this small, mostly Parisian group that formed through distinct affinities in the early 1930s and gave birth to the Union of Modern Artists, whose French acronym is UAM.

In 1908, in Vienna, Adolf Loos (1870–1933), the purists' purist, denounced the decorative aspect of art in his essay *Ornament* und *Verbrechen* ("Ornament and Crime"), an epoch-making manifesto, which would become the foundation of modernism. He was radically opposed to the elegant composite developed by Joseph Hoffmann to reconcile the simplifications of post–Art Nouveau style with Viennese *gemütlichkeit* (amicability). Born in Brno, Moravia, Loos built his most significant architectural work, the Steiner house, in the Austrian capital in 1910. The Steiner house is made of reinforced concrete; its geometric

spaces are spare, pierced with wide windows, and topped with a semicircular flat roof. This intransigence was twenty years ahead of its time. In the meantime, indoor plumbing, the electric light-bulb, the telephone, the radio, the automobile, and aviation, along with significant social progress, had profoundly changed daily life.

However, the fact remains that, despite such progress, the role of the artist needed to be preserved alongside that of the engineer. In a world with rational pretentions, this can be problematic, but never-theless, is essential to quality of life. The problem of design, in those decades of major change, consisted of balancing aesthetics and practicality in products that were pared down to the essentials. It is a continuation of the same debate initiated by the Arts and Crafts movement in the middle of the previous century, though established decorative artists, falling back on values learned from Art Deco, were less prepared to assimilate the profound changes heralded by the terrible economic crisis that was devastating Europe.

OPPOSITE:
View of the living room in Robert Mallet-Stevens's house, Paris, c. 1927.

ABOVE (FROM LEFT TO RIGHT):
Charles Guevrekian, Garden of Water and Light in the Noailles villa, Hyères.

Robert Mallet-Stevens (attributed to), collector's chair made of lacquered steel pipe, 1930. Pompidou Center, Paris.

Charles and Marie-Laure de Noailles with Jean Cocteau and Christian Bérard (in front), 1930.

Robert Mallet-Stevens, chairs
conceived for the swimming pool
of the vicomte de Noailles's villa
in Hyères, 1924.
Pompidou Center, Paris.

OPPOSITE Swimming pool of the
Noailles villa, in Hyères.

Pierre Chareau, front of the Maison de Verre, 1931. Rue Saint-Guillaume, Paris.

OPPOSITE: Pierre Chareau, sitting room of the Maison de Verre, 1931. Paris.

Designed for Dr. Dalsace, this apartment-clinic building is famous throughout the world. The two facades overlooking a courtyard and garden are made of glass tiles, which were revolutionary at the time. Extremely light, this three-story structure still houses its original furniture designed by Pierre Chareau (1883–1950).

In 1920, *L'Esprit Nouveau,* the rationalist French magazine of international constructive art, began working to place the visual arts, music, the sciences, architecture, and industrial production on par with one another. Jazz strains and the gears of machine-age poetics swept modern times far from decorative academicism and its comforts.

In what would become a definitive moment of 1920s modernism, Le Corbusier obtained space for the *Esprit Nouveau* pavilion at the 1925 Exhibition of Modern Decorative and Industrial Arts. His goal in exhibiting a cellular living unit was to demonstrate the radical evolution that could now be applied to collective housing developments, thanks to modern construction techniques. This experimental unit integrated works by Braque, Picasso, Léger, Lipchitz, Gris, and Ozenfant into all of the practical imperatives. Ill-prepared at the time, many visitors took this prophetic vision of the future as a provocation. People spoke of Bolshevism and "hideous nudism," when they weren't accusing the modernists of selling out to Germany, the great enemy of yesterday.

Pierre Chareau, stool in wood
and wrought iron, 1927.

OPPOSITE: Pierre Chareau, detail
of the living room in the Maison
de Verre, Paris, 1931

Another benchmark of twenties modernism was the 1929 International Exhibition in Barcelona, for which Mies van der Rohe constructed the German Pavilion, now referred to as the Barcelona Pavilion. This steel and concrete structure, with floor-to-ceiling glass walls, validated the designer's belief that "less is more." The pavilion also served as a showcase for definitive modern interiors, including van der Rohe's leather-upholstered *Barcelona* chair, which has been produced by Knoll ever since.

That same year, René Herbst (1891–1982), Jean Fouquet (1420–1480), Gérard Sandoz, Jean Puiforcat, Hélène Henry, and several others permanently broke with the Salon des Artistes Décorateurs, the decorative-arts trade show of the day. Instead, they decided to exhibit their work at the Salon d'Automne, which was theoretically only for new trends in the visual arts. They were joined by Le Corbusier and his colleagues, Pierre Jeanneret (1896–1967) and Charlotte Perriand (1903–1999). This visionary triumvirate made a splash with its innovative proposals, which to this day have lost none of their freshness. The distinctive feature of their display, which they termed "outfitting" rather than "decor," was the use of standard compartments, all produced with the same metal framework. Their modular structure allowed spaces to be arranged along dividing walls, like a free-floating spine, separating two rooms with openings on one side or the other, to hold clothing, dishware, books, and miscellaneous items, thus freeing the house from clutter. The furniture was composed of tables whose common component allowed them to be rearranged, and tubular chrome seats, which were light and economical, yet comfortable. Serenity and luminosity made up the prevailing ambiance. Unfortunately, people once again balked. And no partner was found among the industrialists to manufacture these

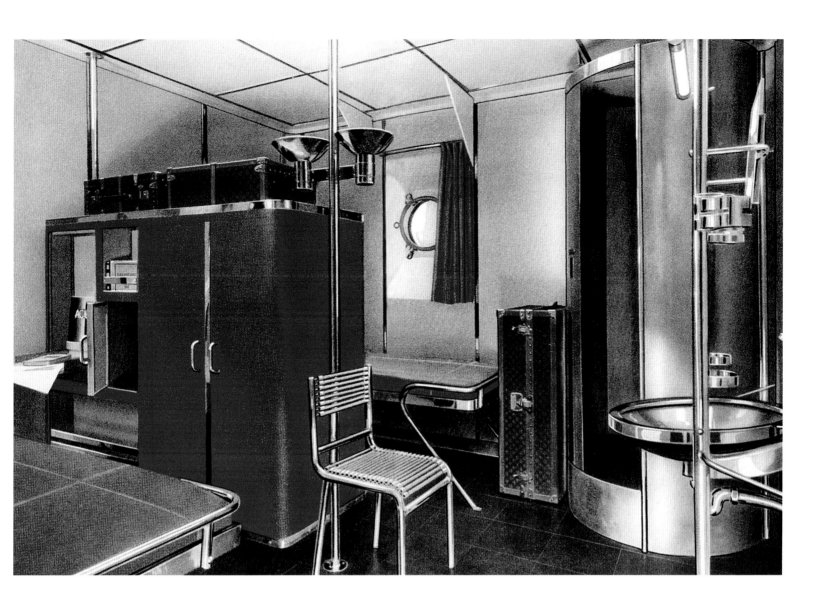

René Herbst, ship's cabin, 1934.

Introduced in 1934 at the Salon d'Automne, this first-class room showcased lightness, durability, and elegance. The amazing modernism successfully unites art and industry. Hélène Henry textiles, Louis Vuitton luggage. Document extracted from Acier *magazine, 1935.*

prototypes. Le Corbusier and his peers would have to wait until the late seventies to finally find a receptive audience. Then, ironically, firms such as Italian furniture designer Cassina rereleased exclusive versions of the prototypes that their creators had intended for mass distribution. Interior designer Andrée Putman (b. 1925) revived several models that had been designed by members of the UAM and never distributed. This would scandalize twentieth-century antique specialists, who had long speculated on the rarity of works left behind by these design pioneers. (Though it would prove to be an unfounded concern, as evidenced by the prices at auctions today.)

The first exhibition of the Union of Modern Artists as such was held in 1930 at the Marsan pavilion on the rue de Rivoli in Paris. Exemplifying the multidisciplinary approach of the more than thirty talents that the venue brought together, founding members such as architects Robert Mallet-Stevens (1886–1945), René Herbst, and Francis Jourdain (1876–1958) rubbed elbows with the engineer Jean Prouvé (1901–1984); poster designer, graphic artist, and illustrator Paul Colin (1829–1985); glassblower Louis Barillet (1880–1948); sculptors such as Gustave Miklos (1913–1967) and Jan and Joel Martel; gold and silversmiths such as Gérard Sandoz and Jean Fouquet; textile designer Hélène Henry; and the iconic Eileen Gray. Then the already famous Pierre Chareau (1883–1950), Gerrit Rietveld, Cassandre, Fernand Léger, Georges Candilis, Bernard Zerfuss, Jean-Charles Moreux, and Louis Sognot joined the original group. All were different, but the UAM created a subtle bond between them, composed of distinct affinities and pronounced dislikes. Until the outbreak of World War II, their exhibitions were aimed at giving the term "modern" renewed significance, i.e., eliminating the gap between art and everyday objects, simplifying daily tasks by streamlining them, and implementing social progress—all the while preventing a lack of resources from reducing the sensibility or the often humor-tinged refinement of the objects. After the Liberation, this nondogmatic ethic led the UAM to join forces with the Salon des Arts Ménagers, as the consumer society began to appear on the old continent. In the 1950s, these pioneers ran the salon's "Useful Forms" division, whose concepts prefigured the design of the next generation. Meanwhile, on the UAM's stands, polymorphic plastic, Lurçat tapestries, Calder mobiles, Atlas rugs, and milking stools coincided with technological innovations such as glulam, airplane propellers, the Thonet chair, and the latest rocket-ship-shaped vacuum cleaner, because while housing was limited and increasingly cramped in a France in the midst of reconstruction, people were still dreaming about the conquest of space.

Charlotte Perriand, dining room presented at the Salon des Artistes Décorateurs, Paris, 1928. Extendable table with swivel armchairs.

Thirties and Forties

Reacting against the abstract designs that had reigned worldwide since the 1930s, the decorative arts made a fresh turn. A blend of neoclassicism, rococo, and lavish modernity, this era of contradictions heralded long-lasting changes.

Emilio Terry
for Jean-Michel Frank,
large mirror with branch
motif, stucco, c. 1930.

OPPOSITE: André Arbus,
dining room for a residence
in île-de-France. Société des
artistes décorateurs pavilion,
1937 exposition.

Stucco table sculpted by Androuson; chairs varnished in white and gold, tapestries based on Paule Marrot; tortoiseshell armoire, prune-colored veneer, and gilded bronze mask by Androuson. Mirror decorated by Paule and Max Ingrand. Ironwork by Gilbert Poillerat. Bas-relief by Paul Belmondo.

The years between the two World Wars promoted divergent and evolving views that emerged out of a period of economic crisis and social upheaval. These aesthetic contrasts and contradictions often muddied the landscape and discouraged overly stringent classification or chronology. The more trends collided or overlapped, the more it appeared silly to judge between ancient and modern, classical and Baroque, representation and abstraction, realism and surrealism. The 1930s marked a new period of sobriety and, moreover, severity, where aesthetic frivolity would be displaced by functionalism.

Many of the dualisms of the era came head-to-head in Europe at the 1937 Exposition Internationale des Arts et Techniques dans la Vie Moderne, held in Paris in front of the new Trocadero Palace. At this exhibition, the pavilions of Nazi Germany and the Soviet Union stood across from each other, heralding the opposition that would soon follow.

Jean-Michel Frank, beauty room
of the Guerlain Institute on the Champs-Élysées.
Trompe-l'œil and painted console
by Christian Bérard, 1939.

Alberto and Diego Giacometti for Jean-Michel Frank, female head table lamp, 1936. Gold-finished plaster.

During this era, a harmony of styles would synthesize traditional forms with the needs of the modern world. From that perspective, Great Britain and the United States have always been more at ease with this period, and they consider its diversity, imagination, and revivals as innovations. Figures such as Lady Colefax, Oliver Messel, Syrie Maugham (the wife of novelist Somerset Maugham), and eccentric photographer and theatrical designer Cecil Beaton, among others, have never lost their influence across the English Channel.

In the United States, which was on the verge of becoming the new world center for the arts, curiosity fueled these conflicting influences in a host of trends whose consumption spared no social category. But as much as the era's new functionalist

aesthetics proliferated, the spirit of consumerism would remain at the helm, illustrating designer Raymond Loewy's dictum "Ugliness doesn't sell."

Since things need a name, this long and complex period, brought back into vogue by antique dealers, enthusiasts on the lookout for new discoveries, and a young generation with no memories of its first incarnation, has recently been christened "forties style." Its revival coincided with postmodernism, a vague

Jean-Michel Frank, armchair, from a pair. Low seat, off-white galuchat leather, Paris, c. 1930.

TOP (FROM LEFT TO RIGHT):
Jean-Michel Frank's house in 1930.
The living room walls are covered with inlaid straw; sofa in natural leather.

Fireplace designed by Alberto and Diego Giacometti for Jean-Michel Frank, with a lamp by Frank and a pair of elephants sculpted by Paul Iribe.

Jean-Michel Frank surrounded by (FROM LEFT TO RIGHT) A. Giacometti, E. Terry, A. Chanaux, and D. Giacometti; (SITTING) Rodocanacchi and Bérard.

Mr. Templeton Crocker sitting
in the living room of the penthouse
he conceived, with decor and
furniture (armchairs, lion skin
on floor, and Moroccan rugs)
by Jean-Michel Frank, 1928.
San Francisco.

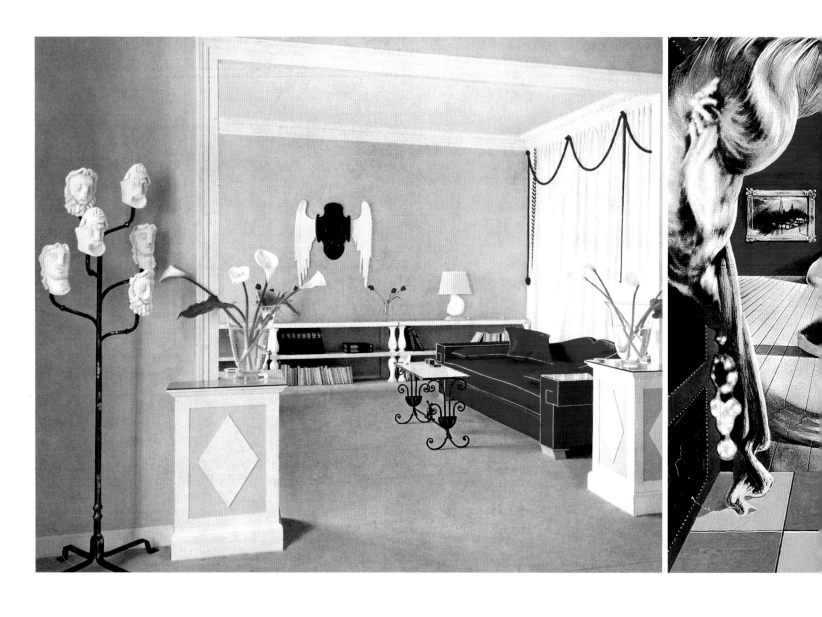

Sonia Batcheff's apartment, decorated by Jean-Charles Moreux, 1939.

Salvador Dalí, *Face of Mae West,* as an apartment, The Art Institute, Chicago, 1934–1935.

Le Corbusier and Carlos de Beistegui, apartment on the Champs-Élysées, c. 1930, Paris.

but vast reexamination of the concept of progress in architecture, perpetrated in the West in the 1980s.

Many French artisans and decorative artists who lived through the Occupation barely missed seeing their works be reinstated in their lifetime by a popularity that has remained constant ever since. The style of the thirties and forties, outside the totalitarian regimes, was intentionally monumental, but generally non-aggressive. Allusions to peace and prosperity and the delightful mythology of secondary regional gods abounded. This harmonious sweet life was barely ever disquieted by a few late borrowings from surrealism.

The dictum for this transitory era was "spirit of succession," an expression used to describe the abundant production of cabinet-

maker André Arbus (1903–1969), among others. Rather than revolutionize domestic furnishing, Arbus turned to the classicism of the eighteenth century for inspiration, without fully adopting its decorative motifs.

Simultanously, his friends Jean-Charles Moreux, of the UAM, and Pierre Barbe, a defender of purism, each worked on an eighteenth-century revival. At the same time, Bolette Natanson drew her inspiration from Greece. Marc du Plantier fused classicism and modernism. Maxime Old was on the verge of heavy-handedness. Louis Sûe was tempted by the theatrical. Emilio Terry's (1890–1969) architecture was metaphysical, and Christian Bérard painted figures in Schiaparelli gowns gliding across lagoonal horizons. Jean Cocteau remains the best storyteller, the fitful poet of those

The austere Swiss architect designed this rooftop apartment on the Champs-Élysées. Its functionalism was quickly transformed by an eccentric millionaire. In a single location, one can see the two extremes of the era.

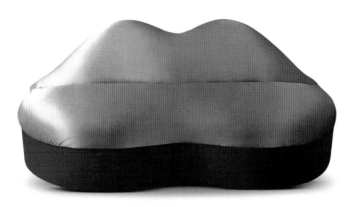

Salvador Dalí, sofa representing the shape of Mae West's lips, 1937.

OPPOSITE: Le Corbusier and Carlos de Beistegui, decor of an apartment on the Champs-Élysées, Paris, c. 1930.

troubled, crisis-fraught years, where artists and designers held on to history as a refence point for their own aesthetic aims.

The most dominant—and arguably the most colorful—personality of Parisian interior architecture between 1932 and 1941 undoubtedly remains Jean-Michel Frank, an unconventional designer whose influence is still widely felt, since many of his designs continue to be popular. Frank, like Chanel in couture, promoted luxury through simplicity rendered with sumptuous materials. His style, which incorporated imagery from such artistic movements as surrealism, was popularized by iconic designs like his couch in the shape of a mouth and his leather club sofa. The furnishings, down to

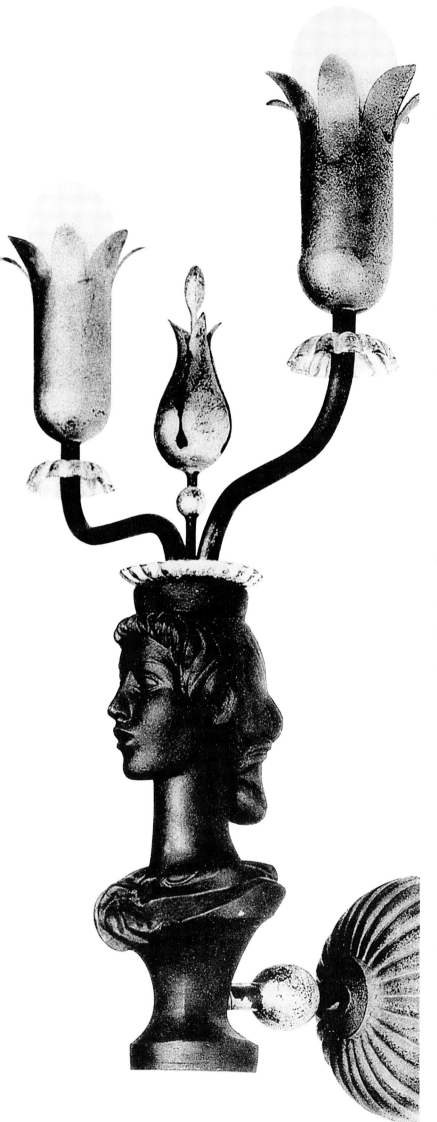

the slightest object, were executed with a level of skill and crafsmanship that made each of them a rarity. With Frank's luxurious yet restrained style—the paradoxical herald of minimalism—one era ended and another began. Following a visit to Frank's home, Cocteau was heard to say, "A charming young man. What a shame he was robbed." René Crevel, the brothers Diego and Alberto Giacometti, Christian Bérard, Salvador Dalí, Marie-Laure de Noailles, Pierre Drieu La Rochelle, numerous South Americans, and the Rockefellers all patronized this unique talent. As World War II approached, fearing persecution, like so many of his contemporaries, Frank emigrated to New York, where he lived until he committed suicide. He was an exile, despite the most promising prospects that opened up before him.

While Europe, struck with economic crisis, unemployment, and political strife, sank deeper and deeper, in New York in 1939, an entirely different World's Fair was opening. It reflected an American way of life that the Old World would not discover until a decade later. In the interim, so many things would change.

Under European influence, American art

did not come into its own until the 1920s. A late Art Deco period slowly developed to the captivating rhythms of swing, destined for a society where novelty and efficiency mattered. Symbolic of that euphoric generation are the top of the Chrysler Building, with its willowy stainless-steel arrows; various hotels and facades in Miami Beach; and New York's Radio City Music Hall and Rockefeller Center, with their dazzling lights, asymmetrical friezes, gilded wrought iron, marble, and sparkling fountains.

It was the era when Austrian émigré Paul Frankl (1887–1958) launched the skyscraper style of purist and cubist-oriented furniture. American designers like Gilbert Rohde (1894–1944) and Donald Deskey (1894–1989) strove to develop the same smooth, brilliant, and abstract aesthetic that was equally appropriate to the home and office. This was symbolized by aluminum, a light, new medium haloed by a prestige conferred by its use in the aeronautics industry. In contrast, Bakelite, a hard, synthetic material, was substituted for costlier ones, such as ivory and ebony, for handles on furniture and teapots. These new materials were also used to

PRECEDING PAGES: Dining room in Daisy Fellowes's hotel, Decor in stucco, glass flooring, glass furniture and glass bead curtains, 1930. Neuilly-sur-Seine.

OPPOSITE: Gilbert Poillerat, female head wall light made of cast iron, c. 1945.

ABOVE: (FROM LEFT TO RIGHT) Herbert List, *Jean Cocteau*, 1944. Chalk drawing on wall.

Gilbert Poillerat, patinated-wrought-iron pedestal table with marble top, exposed in 1943 in the Marsan pavilion.

Mademoiselle Chanel at Her Apartment in the Ritz, illustration by Christian Bérard, published in French *Vogue* in March 1937.

Syrie Maugham, living room of his King's Road house, London, c. 1937.

OPPOSITE: Terrence Harold Robsjohn-Gibbings, dining room of Hilda Boldt Webert's house, Bel-Air, California, 1938.

veneer the laminate furniture distributed under the Formica label. Thus commenced the plastics boom.

In the factory, the compression molding method encouraged designers to simplify their motifs, to create round or aerodynamic shapes. This was the origin of "streamlining," a term applied to the smooth forms and slick surfaces of the modernized kitchen and bathroom, with their shiny new cabinets and appliances. Diners—stainless-steel train-car-shaped restaurants that were delivered, fully equipped, to the intersections of big cities—came to symbolize the use of industrialized materials and streamlining with curved trims and interiors. Manufactured in the same way, after the war brought about advances in technology, were Airstream mobile homes: large, single-hulled, riveted-aluminum structures that rendered the home transportable. On the other end of the spectrum were the European bourgeois, who were still alarmed by the horrors of modernism, particularly the use of industrialized materials.

Often called Depression style, the industrial design that flourished after the Great Depression never stopped spurring

PRECEDING PAGES:
LEFT: Dorothy Draper, lobby
of the Mark Hopkins Hotel,
San Francisco, 1935.
RIGHT: Frances Elkins
and David Adler, library of
the Reed residence,
North Shore, 1930.
Leather sofa and marble
table by Jean-Michel Frank.

consumption in New Deal America. Nevertheless, it generated an aesthetic of its own and eventually spread widely throughout a liberated Europe. At the same time, a purely American, but less anecdotal, style took hold across the Atlantic at the instigation of some great designers and communicators. The most representative of these was the French-born Raymond Loewy (1893–1986), who emigrated to the U.S. in 1929. Over the course of an international career that spanned more than forty years, his agency tackled the redesign of machines, locomotives, and automobiles (including the popular Studebaker coupe); the packaging of Lucky Strike cigarettes; Rosenthal porcelain; and logos for Shell,

Exxon, New Man, and many others. The list of his projects is extensive and included, at the end of Loewy's career, NASA. Though his work never directly extended to domestic architecture or decoration, he bore a strong influence on the environment and the history of style in the latter half of the twentieth century. On both sides of the Atlantic, it was characterized by an unprecedented rise in the standard of living linking economics and the evolution of style.

John Baeder,
Empire Diner, 1976.
Oil on canvas.

OPPOSITE: Raymond Loewy's office, reconstructed for an exposition in 1934 at the Metropolitan Museum of Art, New York.

RIGHT AND FOLLOWING PAGES: Frank Lloyd Wright,
living room and bedroom in the Fallingwater house,
Bear Run, Pennsylvania, 1935.

Scandinavia

Since the beginning of the twentieth century, northern European countries have developed an original style. It is timeless and stands on its own while continuing to embody major international trends.

In both architecture and interiors, Scandinavian designs are often rooted in tradition. Off the beaten path, Scandinavia was nevertheless influential in the late 1930s, as its designers maintained a profound originality and regional character in an environment of international-style modernism and industrial design. Drawing from its geography, wood dominates Scandinavia's warm and functional traditional craftsmanship.

Finnish architect and designer Alvar Aalto (1898–1976) quickly became the key figure in Scandinavian style. Under the influence of Swedish architect Gunnar Erik Asplund (1885–1941), Aalto became imbued with the neoclassical simplification that had pervaded the northern school since the nineteenth century, before moving on to international-style modernism later in his career. His approach was comparable to that of Frank Lloyd Wright. A friend of Gropius and Le Corbusier, Aalto was engaged to build the Finnish pavilion at the 1937 International Exhibition in Paris. At the same time, and more enduringly, he strove to

ABOVE: Alvar Aalto, *Savoy vase*, c. 1967. Blown glass, cast in Azur shape.

OPPOSITE: Alvar Aalto, 1937 house. Noormarkku, Finland.

translate the shapes of Bauhaus tubular chairs into the vast vocabulary of laminated woods, of which he a pioneer.

Respect for a job well done, a clear and accomplished style, a sensuality full of gentle curves, a simplicity that never neglected elegance, and the lure of unknown horizons made Aalto's pieces an important decorative influence in both Europe and the U.S. at the dawn of the 1950s. The warmth of his work, with its generous use of wood and undulating surfaces, seemed a positive alternative to international-style modernism.

Designs from the five Scandinavian countries, and Denmark in particular, would incorporate their histories into the modern style, thus taking on the monikers "Swedish modern" and "Danish modern." Georg Jensen's (1866–1935) silver jewelry; furniture manufactured by Fritz Hansen; and Arne Jacobsen's (1902–1971) iconic *Egg*, *Swan*, and *Ant* chairs are free, sculptural designs that clearly express a poetic interpretation of nature. Another important contributor was lighting designer Poul Henningsen (1894–1967), whose remarkable *Artichoke* ceiling lamp (1956),

RIGHT: Alvar Aalto, 1937 house, Noormarkku, Finland.

a sphere of copper sheets that refract light without glare, is a suspended fixture still fresh today.

The smooth lines introduced by Poul Kjaerholm (1929–1980), Henning Koppel (1918–1981), and artisan designers such as Finn Juhl (1912–1989) and Hans Wegner (b. 1914), along with the colorful abstract textiles produced by several firms and individual weavers, contributed to the public's love of this warmly sober and egalitarian style. It seamlessly merged with other foreign innovations, creating a new living environment for the 1950s.

Although he spent his formative years in the United States, Eero Saarinen (1910–1961), along with Aalto, was dominating the Nordic movement. He was the son of Eliel Saarinen (1873–1950), the influential architect who designed the Helsinki railway station before he emigrated. In addition to his architecture—distinguished by its sinuous shapes—Saarinen's iconic *Tulip* chairs, as well as his aluminum seats covered with white plastic shells, anchored by a central base, have been in production by Knoll since 1956, with great success both commercially and as fine art.

LEFT: Arne Jacobsen, *Egg* chair, 1957.

The Fifties

The second half of the twentieth century, which opened with the liberation of Europe, ushered in profound changes signifying hope. The word "modern" was on everyone's lips, even though it evoked different sentiments.

After World War II, the United States was the richest country in the world. A booming economy, low production costs, and renewed buying power encouraged creativity in design. The era was rich with works by such architects and designers as Charles Eames (1907–1978), Hans and Florence Schust Knoll, George Nelson (1908–1986), and Eero Saarinen, and sculptors such as Isamu Noguchi (1904–1988), whose work included lamps made of paper stretched over a bamboo frame. Also held in great esteem were

Serge Mouille, wall lamp, 1953.

RIGHT: Richard Neutra, Desert House in Palm Springs, designed for Edgar Kaufmann. Palm Springs, California.

Charles and Ray Eames in their 1958 living room. Pacific Palisades, California.

BELOW: Charles and Ray Eames, the famous lounge chair and ottoman, tried out by Dick Hoffman, director of manufacturing at Herman Miller, 1956.

furniture designers such as Harry Bertoia (1915–1978), who was best known for his chairs made of thin metal rods held together with wire mesh. It was no longer possible to doubt the merits of mass production. Now, form quite obviously followed function, and this unity would find its best expression, be it metal, wood laminate, fiberglass, polyester, plastic, foam rubber, or other emerging materials.

One of the finest examples of the alliance between form and function was the luxurious lounge chair designed by Charles Eames in 1956 for his friend, the film director Billy Wilder. The adjustable, molded rosewood lounge chair, mounted on a metal swivel base and equipped with an ottoman and a headrest, combines all the comfort anyone could

OPPOSITE: Living room of the Eames House, Pacific Palisades, California, 1949.

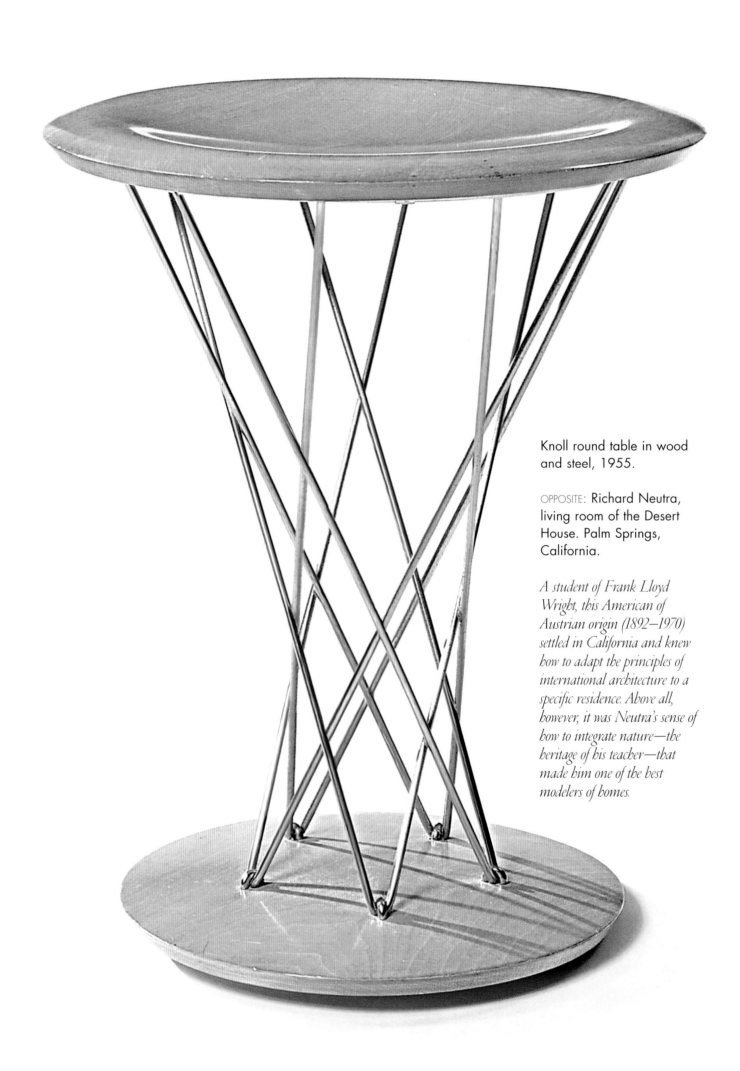

Knoll round table in wood and steel, 1955.

OPPOSITE: Richard Neutra, living room of the Desert House. Palm Springs, California.

A student of Frank Lloyd Wright, this American of Austrian origin (1892–1970) settled in California and knew how to adapt the principles of international architecture to a specific residence. Above all, however, it was Neutra's sense of how to integrate nature—the heritage of his teacher—that made him one of the best modelers of homes.

ask for. Industrially manufactured but patrician in style, with more than a half century of esteem, this great classic has entered the most varied of dwellings. The British easy chairs of the nineteenth century had nothing on this symbol of relaxed affluence.

With the collaborative force of his wife, Ray, Eames became the most famous American designer of his generation. Together, in 1949 they undertook the design of their luminous home in Santa Monica. A model of its genre, the decor was a combination of common building materials, salvaged items, the most diverse collections, and a proliferation of green plants—an eclecticism heralding a new concept of space design that would influence the next generation and further widen the gap between the "total look" of environments reserved for the elite and a broader, much less formal market.

The fifties had fewer uniform trends than any other decade. This was all the more true in that creativity became globalized, relayed by a network of modern communications. Only Eastern Europe, China, and the Third World escaped the effects of style and its influence on consumption.

However, in both America and Europe, in societies in the midst of postwar rebuilding, the divide was constantly widening between the pragmatism imposed by the contingencies of the day and the high style that continued to be reflected in upscale art and decoration magazines such as *House and Garden, Connaissance des arts,* and *L'Œil.* While the American way of life was the stuff of dreams and did spark many changes, particularly in the practical domain, there was a veritable

OPPOSITE: Pierre Koenig, *Case Study House no. 21,* Getty Research Institute, Los Angeles, c. 1950.

Sharp portable television set, c. 1950.

return to "the good old days" in the private sphere. This return to tradition and old-world elegance was reflected in the revival of Parisian haute couture in 1946 to 1947, which brought back a level of taste and craftsmanship that people had thought were gone forever.

Neither film, theater, painting, literature, or the art of living were spared this Neo-Romanticism, whose very excessiveness was a reaction to the rigors of the times. In France, rations were not abolished until 1950. Germany was in ruins. Thanks to the Marshall Plan, Italy began to make up for lost time.

Many of those who had fallen in step with modernism before the war now associated it with the disasters of totalitarianism or confined it to the workaday world. Even if a certain resurgent *joie de vivre* among the most optimistic spurred to espouse an avant-garde boldness, throughout the 1950s distrust made the pendulum swing back and forth between the utilitarian ready-made and an exponentially increasing infatuation with the decrepit charms of the secondhand. Interior decorators were torn between the two extremes of continuing to do custom work for a select clientele and satisfying the aspirations of the new generation that would embody the "Thirty Glorious Years."

Rising consumer demand led to an era of widespread prosperity, higher living standards, and social mobility. The birthrate soared between 1946 and 1964, and peaked in 1957, when a baby was born every seven seconds. Of the thirteen million new homes built in the U.S. in the fifties, 85 percent were in the suburbs.

Sitting room in the apartment decorated by George Geoffrey for Christian Dior, La Muette park, Paris, 1955.

Another new arrival—the television—would also profoundly change domestic habits. The living room became a family room, with a sofa and a dinette. The kitchen would be filled with colorful modern appliances—including dishwashers and refrigerators. Polished wood floors gave way to wall-to-wall carpeting, maintained by a whirlwind vacuum cleaner. Coffered paneling was disappearing beneath fabric or wallpaper, hung high and low. Plant stands, coffee tables, indirect lighting, and magazine racks sprung up, along with ingenious gadgets whose common objective was to promise an easier life, more cheerful surroundings, and a home that radiated domestic bliss.

Hunkered in their fortresses in suburban neighborhoods, the

Stéphane Boudin, sitting room of the duke and duchess of Windsor's mansion, in the Bois de Boulogne, Paris, c. 1950.

Blue and silver salon with Louis XVI wood trim and furnishings. This sunlit room, decorated in the early 1950s by the director of the house of Jansen, Stéphane Boudin, sought to re-create a pale atmosphere for Wallis Windsor, evoking the style of Marie-Antoinette. Conventional Louis XVI decor was adopted for these beautiful living quarters, and the "hideous nudity" of postwar furniture was rejected.

273

Marcel Rochas' design
studio, 1954.

world's fortunate were nevertheless troubled by this wave of efficiency and convenience straight out of the 1920s, whose fallout was influencing their own lifestyle, and their own domestic notions. A desire to capture the *Zeitgeist* while preserving diversified elements of the past, the availability of reliable resources for the craftsmen who still possessed the creative skills to use them, and regained affluence were favorable conjunctions that would allow culture to embrace the so-called minor arts, leading to the last golden age of decoration on both sides of the Atlantic.

In England, the glamor of stately homes, the omnipresence of nature in the form of flowers, and an affected taste for cozy charm came together and generated a style that still has consid-

erable influence through what is now known as Cottage style. But it is worthwhile to note that this reuse of the dilapidated and exaltation of the cozy did not preclude inventiveness. Emblematic of the cottage look is John Fowler (1906–1977). An expert on traditional styles, Fowler partnered with Virginia-born Nancy Lancaster, owner of Colefax & Fowler, to develop a style emphasizing the faded, the worn, the slightly touched-up, by infusing eccentric elements into the overly authoritarian ambiance of the Victorian cottage and the many international variants invented for it. In this eclectic mix, hand-crocheted lacework rubbed elbows with Highland tartans; Regency or Empire mahogany was painted white and positioned next to wicker, and of course, floral

chintz was a dominating pattern. These decors popped with fresh colors and were housed inside Palladian-influenced structures, perfumed with potpourri.

The Georgian architecture popular in the U.S. went perfectly with the furnishings of English designer Terrence Harold Robsjohn-Gibbings (1905–1976). With a love of ancient culture as his sole source of inspiration, he was able to combine his Nordic roots and a sense of modernity like no one else's into light, airy groupings, free of decorative imitation or knickknacks.

In France, the Liberation was an opportunity for an entire society that had lived through the opulence of the thirties to return to their prewar habits, which they believed had been temporarily interrupted. Parisian fashion and decor combined to reconstruct a brilliant atmosphere, as reported by the press and led by several noted socialites. Their less-well-off imitators convinced themselves that, with a few concessions, everything would go on as before, even though square footage and standards of living were ineluctably reduced. Now there were fewer family estates than rustic cottages, fewer palaces in Venice than secondary residences; it was the Riviera instead of the castle in Sologne and the apartment on the edge of the Bois de Boulogne

instead of the old mansion. Family heirlooms (or supposed family heirlooms) were accompanied by flea-market finds. The Louis XVI piece was spruced up, the pedestal table was skirted, and the old torch holders were electrified. The Napoleon II piece was deemed hideous but amusing. The Belle Epoque was free for all. Art Deco style was still reserved for the offices of provincial businessmen, and modern style for the working class or the progressives. Antique dealers revived Boulle furniture, Dutch copper chandeliers, and Aubusson carpets. They would soon invent the High Renaissance style that embraced a vast panorama, from the Renaissance cabinet to the farmhouse table. An enlightened crowd suddenly stood in opposition to their Louis XVIII style. It drew its inspiration from the designs of utopian architects of the late eighteenth century, such as Claude Nicolas Ledoux, whom Cuban-born architect and designer Emilio Terry, with the support of his patron Carlos de Beistegui, reinterpreted in his all-too-rare creations and imaginary architecture, followed by great decorators such as Georges Geffroy, Victor Grandpierre, the Jansen firm, and several others who defined this simultaneously virile and affected style. During the same period, this stood in contrast to the freewheeling femininity of Madeleine Castaing (1894–1992), the high priestess of Romantic decoration. Her very personal choices, using the most original elements of Empire through Louis Philippe–style decor, where the shadow of Madame Bovary sometimes crossed that of Scarlett O'Hara in a mixture of ceramic pans, bayadere stripes, caned latticework, and immaculate voile fabrics, had considerable influence on new apartments whose fortunate owners found them lacking in

Jean Royère, eight-armed
lamp, Persian model,
c. 1950.

"Pigalle" brasserie designed
by Gridaine, Paris, c. 1950.

*Under American influence after
the Liberation, many European
cafés adopted an asymmetrical
and naively futuristic style that
their owners welcomed with more
goodwill than discretion, accepting
futurism as the promise of
a new era ahead.*

Line Vautrin, convex mirror,
c. 1950

soul. Madame Castaing had plenty of soul to spare. She lived to be almost 100, enough years to see her style revived by several young people on the Left Bank, which she herself never really left.

The charming retroism cultivated in both France and England during the latter half of the twentieth century did not preclude laudable efforts at modernization. Furnishings that reflected the rigorous standards of reconstruction in the two countries generated the utility style in England, promoted by the Utility Furniture Company. This consisted of inexpensive, cheerful, practical furniture to meet an emergency need, combining modern American and Scandinavian-influenced designs with a hint of Arts and Crafts. But those for whom it was intended often found it too plain. The 1946 Britain Can Make It Exhibition, organized in an effort to improve and promote British designs, was nevertheless a brilliant success.

Encouraged by the public authorities, the French furniture industry saw the return of some of the great prewar woodworkers. They met the needs of ministries, companies, shipping

lines, and hotels. André Arbus was still there, as were Leleu, Spade, and Dominique. Jean Pascaud (1903–1996), Jacques Dumond (1906–1988), Jacques Quinet (b. 1918), several unconventional women such as Colette Guéden (1905–2001) and Suzanne Guiguichon (1900–1985), ironworkers like Subes (1891–1970) and Poillerat (1902–1988), and others prolonged the tradition that would be swept aside by the revolts of the sixties.

Artisanry was especially embodied by a designer who teemed with ideas and wit: Jean Royère (1902–1981). Although he also addressed a privileged clientele—residents of the Riviera, the Champs-Élysées, Beirut, and the Middle East, as well as many

Jean Royère, layout for the office of a Brazilian airline director, 1955–1960.

A Le Havre native, this decorator of legendary fantasy arrived in Paris in 1931, where his career took off with a series of public and private appointments that Royère generally designed down to the last detail. In the 1950s, his career took on an international dimension with work for big clients who were smitten with his innovating ideas. Many of his models (such as the one shown above) are devoid of people and evoke the atmosphere of the comic books of the times, such as Spirou.

Jean Royère.
Eléphantea chair,
Musée des Arts décoratifs,
Paris, c. 1939.

OPPOSITE: Jean Royère,
living room with
cast-iron Claustra, 1953–1954.
Polar Bear model wood sofa
and chair, covered in wool.

Charlotte Perriand and
Jean Prouvé, library for the
Maison de la Tunisie, 1953.

OPPOSITE: Herbert Krenchel
bowl, 1953.

wealthy South Americans—he constantly tinged his work with a futurism where humor combined with inventiveness. And this loose cannon did so with a freedom that assured him a place on the margins, much like Jean-Michel Frank in the thirties.

Originally intended for a broad audience, the industrial design born in Germany in the 1920s continued its progression in France at the instigation of the wood industries, department stores, institutions, and progressive circles. Jean Prouvé gave his full measure as a designer and engineer of tools for folding sheet steel, bending plywood, and giving new shapes to light alloys. They were based on standardization and aimed at meeting urgent needs, and so were ordered in increasing numbers, inspiring an ideal of social generosity. In the 1980s, speculators in contemporary antiques diverted such then-outmoded furnishings from their original purpose, making them collectors' items. Those of Charlotte Perriand, very similar to those of Prouvé, experienced the same fate. And yet there was an entire group, including René Gabriel, Marcel Gascoin, Mathieu Matégot, Pierre Guariche, Joseph André Motte, and Michel Mortier, who endeavored to breathe new life into output that was already heralding the French design explosion of the 1960s.

However, nothing was comparable to the boom in Italian creativity in postwar Europe. Driven by an industry concentrated in Milan and promoted by large-scale triennial events started by the prolifically inventive Achille (1918–2002) and Pier Giacomo Castiglioni (1913–1968), the design boom in Italy was a veritable renaissance of workmanship and technical prowess. Well beyond the confines of pure functionality, it was lyricism that carried the day, with organic shapes, exaggerated treatments, and exuberant energy.

Piero Fornasetti (1913–1988) drew his inspiration from surrealism for his silkscreen prints, furnishings, textiles, and accessories with architectural motifs and incongruous figures. Paolo Venini (1895–1959) created chandeliers of Murano glass, while Lino Sabatini (b. 1925) Vittorio Gregotti (b. 1927), Lodovico Meneghetti (1926), and Giotto Stoppino (b. 1926) worked together, in the long tradition of craftsmanship, to invent a new style of woodworking. Osvaldo Borsani (1911–1985) and the Tecno company produced endlessly inventive furniture, including recliners with complex mechanisms. Marco Zanusso (b. 1968) conducted the first experiments with latex foam for Pirelli.

By the end of the 1950s, the Italian peninsula would become the world's leading exporter of contemporary furnishings. Decoration, although

FOLLOWING PAGES:
LEFT: Jean Prouvé, Anthony chair in metal and molded plywood, 1954.
RIGHT: Jean Prouvé, Compass desk. Folded-steel sheet metal and wood, 1953.

Born in Nancy in 1901, the architect of the folded-sheet-metal curtain wall played an influential role in the industry in the 1930s by advocating a systematic return to standardization, particularly in the production of attractive and inexpensive light metal furnishings destined for community use.

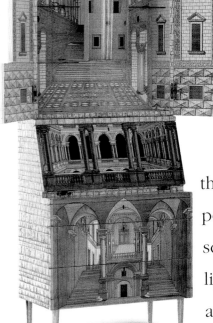

Piero Fornasetti, *Architettura* chest inspired by a Gio Ponti design, 1948.

Gio Ponti and Piero Fornasetti jointly designed several items of furniture whose originality lies in the impression on metal or wood of collages with graphic motifs from ancient architectural engravings. This very imaginative corner desk was exhibited at the first postwar Triennale in Milan.

OPPOSITE: Carlo Mollino, interior of the Casa Mollino, Turin, 1960.

the word was rarely used, followed the same progression as architecture. Both worked in the service of a mobile, aspirational society that was eager to assert itself through furniture and products, rather than just the remains of its glorious past.

The great figure of this bel canto was Gio Ponti (1891–1979). Architect, painter, designer, sculptor, and founder of the magazines *Domus* and *Stile,* this one-man band left behind an opus of astounding variety. From the colossal to the most modest, from collections of Ginori porcelain manufactured in the 1930s to the construction of sky-scrapers, factories, hospitals, and museums, to the design of light fixtures, furniture, and silverware, to theatrical costumes and the graphics in his magazines, nothing escaped this pro-tean genius to whom all of northern Italy is beholden for thirty years of modernism. He also left behind two reference works, one entitled "Architecture is a Crystal," in which he wrote, "A house is a part of our life. It is the vessel in which our happy and unhappy hours elapse. It is the temple of our noblest thoughts. It should be neither in style nor go out of style." From a pronounced liking for ornamentation to the strictest rationalism, he was a foun-tain of essential forms and refined details where nothing was extraneous. But while Ponti remains the icon of Italian creativity in the mid-twentieth century, it was Turin native Carlo Mollino (1905–1973), atypical and solitary, who embodied the Baroque. Architect, decorator, and furniture designer, he was also a race car driver and aviation enthusiast. This led him to conduct research on the aerodynamics of shapes. Be it an aircraft project, race car design, building structure, interior, or piece of furniture, Mollino, master

of the free form, made no distinction. At the same time, he was an educator and wrote several scientific and critical essays. He also left behind a photographic opus with strong erotic connotations. The anthropomorphic inspiration of many of his creations leaves no doubt as to the nature of his primary obsession.

Philip Johnson,
Hodgson House, New Canaan, Connecticut.
Furniture by Florence Schust Knoll, 1951.

One name, like a password, made the rounds from the 1950s to the 1960s. It served as a bridge between generations. Knoll was much more than a trademark; it was a sign of civilization. A few pieces in an empty room suffice to set the stage. The artistic quality of each piece gives it a place in space and unites it with every period and every function.

The adventure began in New York in 1946, when Hans Knoll (1914–1955), the son of a German furniture manufacturer, married Florence Schust, an insightful art student with ties to many designers. They created Knoll Associates, bringing together Bauhaus renegades such as Marcel Breuer (1902–1981) and Ludwig Mies van der Rohe, who had fled Nazi Germany, with artists such as Roberto Matta (1911–2002) and Harry Bertoia, and architects like Eero Saarinen. There were few items in the catalog, but each was so harmoniously designed, with so much precision and refinement, that Knoll became the go-to firm for both designers and consumers.

Florence Schust Knoll storage cabinet, c. 1955.

In 1952, when the company arrived in Saint-Germain-des-Prés, all eyes were on the new design. It was a hit. Mrs. Knoll stripped down her showroom, aimed spotlights at a few stylized groupings, launched a line of abstract fabrics, personally designed a sofa and several glass and steel pieces with basic lines, and was met with incontrovertible and soon international success. Subsequently, the company specialized in high-end office furnishings. But the refined crafting of the seating and the cachet of the brand name continue to find favor among a bourgeoisie enchanted to have its old furniture rub elbows with great contemporary classics.

Florence Schust Knoll sofa and Eero Saarinen table, 1954.

Sixties and Seventies

For a whole generation—the first born from the baby-boom—the future became a reality during the 1960s with new materials, new technologies, and a new art of living. Thanks to design, the consumer society invented a playful decor with limitless horizons.

In Europe, the twenty years following the Liberation was a period of reconstruction and profound restructuring. During these years, the United States, however, expanded its sphere of influence in many areas of innovation, from the conquest of space to the arts, architecture, and design. The Future—embodied in the imagination of Jules Verne—took shape during this final third of the twentieth century. Utopian

ABOVE: Philippe Barbier, Diabolo stool, 1969–1970. Musée des Arts décoratifs, Paris.
RIGHT: John Lautner and Arthur Elrod, Elrod House, Palm Springs, 1968. Rug, Edward Fields; sofa, Martin Brattrud.

ABOVE: David Hockney,
*American Collectors
(Fred and Maria Weisman)*,
1968. Acrylic on canvas.

CENTER: Courcelle and
Pechenard sitting room.

visions conveyed ingenuity and euphoria, which were counte-red by prophets of doom. Decor and furnishings reflected this cohabitation, with its conquests and its contradictions, resulting in a versatile style that single-handedly summarized an obsession with change. Simplified and stylized forms became popular, often associated with dreams of a high-tech space-age future. But this time, it was less a matter of satisfying a set of specific needs than of satiating diffuse desires, illustrated by the accele-ration of fashion; in the 1970s, baby boomers turned 20.

With unprecedented independence—and a keen awareness of its impact—youth subculture imposed its ideals and collective voice. Higher standards of living, an increase in leisure time

and mobility fostered a no-holds-barred creativity. The English term "design," which had previously been used solely in an industrial context, passed into the everyday language.

In a decisive era in the history of style, over just a few short years a society still entrenched in traditional customs initiated mass consumerism and a counterculture of its own. Carried along by a musical wave that benefited from the invention of the LP and the 45-RPM record in the late forties, pop culture was on the march; its leaders would soon be considered the new authorities of both culture and style. The shrewdest manufacturers engaged the skills of designers in order to anticipate trends as fashion entered design. It was no longer enough just to

produce; it was necessary to please. Whereas the modernism of the thirties championed a moral code, the modernism of the sixties asserted the pleasure of instant gratification.

Between tradition and modernity, the surroundings of the privileged class strove to reconcile these new realities. For example, Francis Spar, the editor-in-chief of *Connaissance des arts*, wrote in 1973, "It's over. We no longer live in the decor of the past...The inventory of current habits, needs, and desires is not simple. However, we can attempt to tame it, without claiming to favor any particular side. We no longer want to feel confined; groups form differently (for talking, watching television, etc.); tolerance allows more laid-back sitting positions (we have a greater need for relaxation); domestic help is gradually disappearing; we want to and can listen to music everywhere; it is possible to live in bright light, even at night; many objects are manufactured to make life easier and more pleasant; vivid colors pervade our daily life; there are all sorts of materials with multiple virtues: shiny, matte, hard, soft, washable; we have a great need of nature and natural 'things'; we love change." The dual concept of free time and space now controlled the layout of the home.

In old buildings, partition walls came down, windows were opened, decorative moldings and fireplaces disappeared. Thick carpeting, sometimes with geometric patterns, uniformly covered wood floors. Indirect lighting replaced suspended fixtures. The family room replaced the former living-dining room combination. Admittedly, people were already lamenting the fact that craftsmanship was dying out, though mass-produced items were a tempting substitute. To escape their uniformity, and to ward off the aggressions of the modern world without sacrificing its conveniences, a keen infatuation with the exotic, or simply kitsch, evolved during the sixties. Thus, television sets, hi-fi systems, coffee tables, and deep sofas rubbed elbows with primitive art, rustic furnishings, and Pop Art paintings. Simple,

BELOW: Verner Panton, Living Tower, 1968–1969. Wood covered in "Tonus" fabric (90 percent pure new wool and 10 percent Helanca).

organic forms predominated. It was a matter of giving the impression that an individual's environment was more accessible and informal, less subject to principles and codes, and that theoretically, anything was possible. More than ever, simplicity put itself forward as the last refuge of complicated people. Just as the work of Jean-Michel Frank is essential to understanding the sensibility of the thirties, so too the work of David Hicks (1929–1998), another independent

spirit of society decor, subtly summarized the aspirations of his contemporaries. In 1954, this elegant scion of an English family preferred to decorate his mother's house than to pursue a military career. *House and Garden* magazine was the first to feature the new style, defined by three key features: the use of a contrasting and often audacious palette, a remarkable talent for assembling objects from a wide variety of sources, and a virtuosic handling of textiles. In addition to interiors, Hicks would become a highly influential textile designer, dressing houses from top to bottom, most of which the industry media would present as models. This son-in-law of Lord Mountbatten, who was later knighted by the queen, understood better than any of

BELOW: Model sitting on an inflatable chair by Italian designers Johnatan De Pas, Donato D'Urbino, Paolo Lomazzi, and Carla Scolari, 1968.

OPPOSITE: Verner Panton, Panton chair, 1967. GFK reinforced with fiberglass, Pompidou Center, Paris.

his predecessors that, in the future, decoration would become synonymous with publicity. The consequence of such visibility was that many individuals who were trying to find their own style imitated Hicks, sometimes without even realizing it. Between references to the past and the mod designs of the sixties, interior designers such as François Catroux, David Mlinaric, Geoffrey Bennison, and John Stefanidis flourished.

In French cities, antique shops sprang up everywhere; outside the cities, weekend flea markets became a destination. The more cities were surrounded with concrete, the more people yearned for the past. As design became increasingly

accessible, objects of the past gained in value. The most audacious favored Art Nouveau and Art Deco. In addition to identifying with these pioneering periods, which had been losing favor, young collectors could smell a bargain. Their intuition, which would later prove accurate, united design with antiques.

Other innovations broke with the continuity of traditional decoration. Increasingly repudiated, decoration was replaced by the term "interior design." In addition to flexibility and spatial restructuring, the industry's most notable change occurred through color. Long confined to a more natural and muted spectrum, homes adopted audacious hues inspired by a new generation of painters. Brilliant color combinations dominated: red and black, orange and bright green.

Lighting also evolved, at times inundating rooms with adjustable spotlights borrowed from the film industry. On other

occasions, lights were dimmed, creating mood and velvety nests. Furniture often took on unconventional qualifiers: stackable, foldable, disposable, interchangeable, nonflammable, and even inflatable were adjectives suddenly applied to interiors that emphasized functionality and accessibility. Technology adapted new materials to traditional shapes, which metamorphosed accordingly. Plastic, the most significant, was generously used for furnishings from chairs to lamps. Malleable to all desires, in the sixties plastic became the ruling material of an industry that, if it could not abolish all inequalities, could at least modify the differences.

Quasar, an engineering student, developed huge inner tubes made of polyvinyl chloride, better known as PVC. Abundantly copied, Quasar's inflatable seats, which imitated structures developed by the sculptor Bernard Quentin, bore witness to the

ABOVE: Pierre Paulin's Paris loft, rue du Faubourg-Saint-Antoine.

BELOW: Pierre Paulin, Ribbon chair, produced by Artifort after 1965.

Christian Daninos,
chair, 1968.

OPPOSITE: François
Catroux, Parisian
apartment, c. 1960.

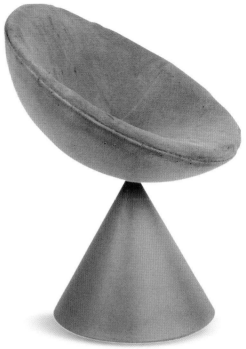

era's slightly inflated hedonism, where relaxation and pleasure were paramount.

Steel yielded to many uses, especially on large surfaces. Industrial glass made use of deceptive transparencies. Lucite and other upscale synthetics (including brick veneer), optical-illusion mosaics, and multifaceted mirrors rivaled draperies and wallpaper as replacements for traditional paneling and moldings. Paper dresses and cardboard furniture were created for young people, for secondary residences (a concept that continued to expand), or just for the fun of it. Saving space, increasing storage, and redefining the function of each room were characteristics of a period that focused on being "with it." Young designers actively expressed this playful spirit.

The boutique was the new offering in retail, and the most dynamic companies invented their own settings for expressing the spirit of conquest. In 1965, the popular French chain store Prisunic and its artistic director Denise Fayolle launched the first

OPPOSITE: Gae Aulenti, interior architecture of an apartment in Milan, 1965. Canvas, Roy Lichtenstein. Herd of sheep, François-Xavier Lalanne, 1965.

ABOVE (FROM LEFT TO RIGHT): Michel Boyer, apartment in the Place des Victoires. Ceiling by sculptor Guy de Rougemont, 1970. Paris.

André Courrèges, white plastic shades, 1965.

Verner Panton C1 chair, 1969. Foam, vinyl, and steel, issued by Pluslinje.

mail-order catalog in France, offering attractive and inexpensive furniture and accessories designed by young designers such as Terence Conran and Marc Held. In 1973, Terence Conran opened his first Habitat store. White wood, charm and color, pretty linens, notebooks, Pop and shock art—all were available and accessible. It was the department store combined with the charm of the fashionable boutique. Conran, its designer, invented a new way of selling and arousing a desire for furnishings at a lower cost. For several generations, shopping at Habitat meant starting out optimistically in life.

Iconic designs like the Kleenex box and the flowered duvet cover replaced traditional items like hand-stitched tea towels and the sacrosanct white trousseau as symbols of the day.

When he was not dreaming of taking off with all his belongings on his back, the fashionable revolutionary was living on the floor of his studio, which was often organized into several levels. Oriental-style sofas reflected this horizontality, and as a sign of equality, most Western women began wearing pants. To live happy, live lying down: one of the most innovative seats for accommodating the posture of the period was the Sacco beanbag chair, a flexible, pear-shaped bag containing several million tiny polystyrene beads, which, to this day, is still in production. In that same spirit, Roberto Matta's Malitte Seating System, a set of modular jersey-covered foam seats, was created to function as a colorful wall sculpture when not in use. And Pierre Paulin (b. 1927), one of the most prolific French designers of the time, designed Déclive, a flexible spiral chair whose rolls were assembled with an articulated aluminum chain. Even more radical, Olivier Mourgue (b. 1939) invented a flying carpet chair. In this case, the chair was not lowered; it was the carpet that was raised, revealing various adjustable backrests covered with long tufts of wool.

The world was being remade as people contemplated ceilings painted purple or decorated with clouds and rainbows. Pop Art, which originated in England and then developed in the United States, propagated hyperrealistic imagery borrowed from cartoon strips, advertising signs, the film industry, and the most sizzling current events.

BELOW: Franco Teodoro, Cesare Paolini and Piero Gatti, *Sacco* beanbag chair, 1968.

ABOVE: Exterior view of Roger Vivier's apartment,
Quai d'Orsay, Paris, 1970.

Roger Vivier, great hall,
Quai d'Orsay, Paris, 1970.
Bodhisattva; Louis XV chair
covered in black leather;
Mies van der Rohe (Knoll)
Barcelona chair; bronze
table from the end of the
seventeenth century.
Poliakoff painting (LEFT) and
an Egyptian ibis on the table
(RIGHT).

Homogeneity was not a concern during those outrageous times, when it was "forbidden to forbid." The British drew inspiration for their fashions from this concept, while the French theorized. The Italians, in the midst of an economic boom, strove to find more practical applications.

Italian design would emerge as the most innovative, with Vico Magistretti, Mario Bellini, Afra and Tobia Scarpa, Gaetano Pesce, Joe Colombo, the visionary Ettore Sottsass for Olivetti (b. 1917), and architect Gae Aulenti (b. 1927) as important influences. Scandinavians Eero Aarnio (b. 1932) and Verner Panton (1926–1998), the Archizoom Group, Studio 65, Superstudio, and Richard Sapper

Billy Baldwin,
Woodson Taulbee
apartment,
c. 1965.

(for Artemide) were just a few of the strong personalities who, in those years, successfully redesigned daily life.

In the seventies, caution urged a progressive fallback to safe values. The chaotic events of the sixties, especially war and social change, seemed destined to continue. In clothing as in furnishings, this translated into a return to natural materials and durable investments. Disillusionment with government, burgeoning civil rights and women's rights movements, and a heightened concern for the environment would define the era. Style increasingly reflected this loss of confidence by rejoining the romantic flight to distant horizons. The early decades of the century, which had undoubtedly passed too quickly, were viewed by many as a golden age. *The Great Gatsby,* Marlene Dietrich, Mickey Mouse, and even the Long March of Chairman Mao were some of the iconic symbols that reappeared like so many antidotes to modernity. Artists like Roy Lichtenstein, Andy Warhol, and David Hockney; styles such as Arman's "smashing" and César's "crushing"; and the

David Hicks, interior of Stavros Niarchos's apartment, Grosvenor Square, London, 1972.

ABOVE: David Hicks, small lounge designed for Selfridges, lacquered wall in shades of red, London, 1969.

OPPOSITE: John Stefanidis, living room of a peculiar house, 1970. Monumental bronze by Rouillet; Mobilier International sofa.

wave of psychedelic style, retro style, kitsch and its aesthetic of garishness came to define this era of social protest and questioning of ideals.

Alongside these diverse design directions was a proliferation of bamboo furniture, Indian fabrics, and all sorts of Asian and Chinese imports. These design aesthetics became popular as the nonviolence of Eastern religion served as a response to the war and a disillusionment with the Establishment.

There was talk of anti-objects, a reference to the readymade of Marcel Duchamp, who was undoubtedly one of the most influential artists of the century. Surrealism was revisited, allowing for all sorts of appropriations and unexpected encounters. And

there was nothing like a flea market to supply this big hodgepodge of symbolism. When it came to clothing and decor, people combed these markets for unusual objects, vaudeville props, and furnishings from the Roaring Twenties. It was a new look that went quite well with the remains of the hippie movement, the furnishings created by artists like Claude and François Xavier Lalanne, Allen Jones, Philippe Hiquily, Guy de Rougemont, and Frank Gehry; with the drapings and spangles of Zandra Rhodes; and equally well with the illusions of op art and the sophistication of kinetic art. In the seventies, everything was grist for combating the grayness of daily routine, the moroseness of conformity, the excesses of capitalism—a word that was all the rage—until "free enterprise" replaced it in the next decade.

Great hall in Henri Samuel's hotel, 1980.
Rue du Faubourg-Saint-Honoré, Paris.

The famous Paris decorator introduced artistic creations then in fashion into eighteenth century spaces. Rougemont's low Clouds *table in steel and chrome;* Skittles *in gilded brass and agate plates, sculpted by Hiquily.*

Paradoxically, this claim of marginality went hand in hand with experimentation of new techniques and materials: polyurethane houses and furniture, geodesic domes, habitats remotely inspired by the space program, which bore its influence on the designs of the era. Alterative forms of living also emerged, and were inspired by art and technology.

Thus, the sixties and seventies would end in a decor of ruins and recession, but in this case it was the ruins of the future. Not to worry. People were already talking about postmodernism.

Jean-Pierre Raynaud, music room, 1978–1979.

FOLLOWING PAGES: Jean-Pierre Raynaud, greenhouse, 1983.

Begun in 1969 and destroyed in 1993, this house was designed from a basic white square as a work in its own right, valued by Jean-Pierre Raynaud as a voluntary prison of space for meditation. All of Paris admired this economy of design and materials until the artist decided to get rid of it in 1993. Its destruction was the focal point of a happening followed by an exhibition.

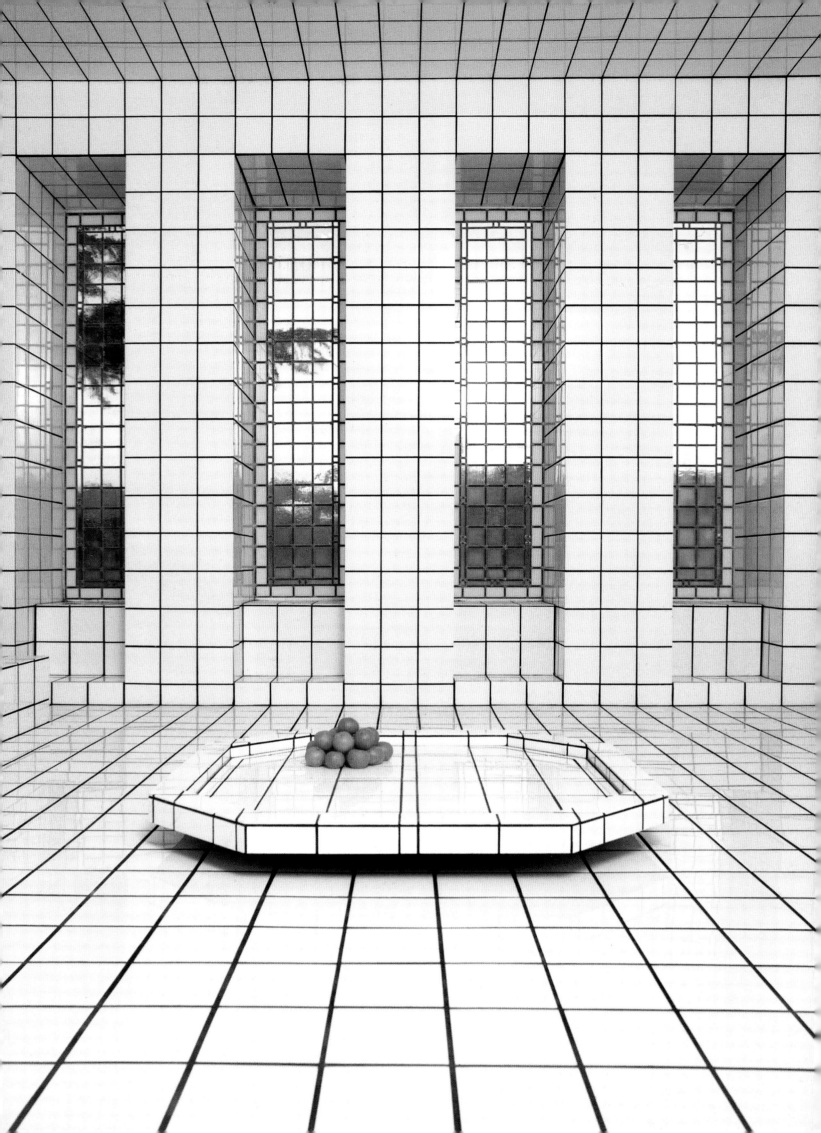

End of the Century

From post-modernism to minimalism, through kitsch and neoclassicism, decor at the end of the twentieth century showed a clear preference for a mélange of styles. During this period, a new style emerged from all the others.

By the 1980s, the twentieth century had entered its final phase. The consumption curve, mirrored by the design curve, had reached its apogee. The stock market was euphoric. Fashion was all the rage. While there was once a time when the history of style was measured in centuries, its progress accelerated into shorter overlapping periods.

With the 1980s, a thousand years of history had ended, along with the modern world as it had been imagined circa 1900. Hence, this suspended period was christened "postmodernism" and attempted to imagine the ruins of the future. Launched by critic Charles Jencks in the late 1970s and then rehashed and appropriated ad nauseum, the term "postmodernism" implies less a rejection of the major trends of modernism than an amused mistrust of its great theories.

The period chose a beautiful mirror through which to view the circular game of the centuries—sometimes focusing on its past, at the risk of falling into it; sometimes fleeing forward in an atmosphere of apocalypse. Between the old palazzo and the

Bed designed by
François-Xavier Lalanne, for
Jacques Grange's apartment,
Paris, 1980.

*The Lalanne furniture gave
great fantasy to interiors
designed during the last decades
of the twentieth century.*

Gabban O'Keefe,
entrance of Madame Pierre
Schlumberger's apartment,
Paris, 1993. A portrait of a
cat by Andy Warhol hangs
above the cement staircase.
Marble floor, steel columns,
and Murano glass lamp.

boxing ring, between creative recovery and barbaric splendor, the history of style and the universe of signs were brewed. All the while, irrationally, the borders between art forms blurred.

With the 1980s came the rebirth of historicism. Excessive decoration was back in style, with randomness occupying an important place, even if it was carefully organized. Alberto Pinto, Jacques Garcia, Peter Marino, Albert Hadley, Mark Hampton, Mario Buatta, Alain Demachy, François-Joseph Graf, Jacques Grange, and Pierre Passebon were some of the interior designers who flew the world over to decorate the lairs of personalities who were often powerful and always concerned

with maintaining their anonymity. Always ready to feed on the latest trends, those who had enthusiastically taken up this design mishmash in the seventies returned to nineteenth-century bourgeois eclecticism—all the more so as bric-a-brac seemed more accessible and more relaxed than traditional nineteenth-century references. Paradoxically, the mosaic of cosmopolitan styles pandered to a trend toward staying at home and retreating inward, which seized hold of the privileged when confronted with the upheavals of novelty. Cocooning, or adopting an insular lifestyle, would become a popular response to the excesses of the eighties.

Atelier of
Loulou de la Falaise
in Montparnasse, 1978.

The genius of Yves Saint Laurent transformed this modest artist's studio, taking inspiration from Jean Cocteau's film Beauty and the Beast, *the title of which sums up his course.*

Boutique hotels, luxury shops, and fashion designer showrooms (commercial/private hybrid spaces) became relay stations for the new trends on display. Design became a strategy in branding. And new decoration magazines, with strong advertising support, shared this art of living with an increasingly broad audience.

While they had long been in opposition, in the 1980s old and new merged to the point that it was no longer possible to tell them apart. This collage of past and present benefited museums, where attendance figures skyrocketed. In the wake of Paris's Pompidou Center, new cultural institutions emerged in city centers. Many acquired departments devoted to fashion, design, photography, and advertising—disciplines that celebrated popular culture and had become part of the twentieth-century art market—alongside their collection of paintings and sculptures. The major auction houses, with Sotheby's in the lead, did much to promote this new type of valuable objects. Silver prints, old advertisements, design prototypes, and travel trunks became objects for decoration and investment.

The sociologist, the anthropologist, the psychologist, and the visual artist became assistants to the postmodern decorator, who himself became a media observer and communications consultant.

Despite its penchant for knickknacks, postmodernism was able to adapt to the most monumental of structures. From that perspective, the inauguration in 1982 of the AT&T building (now the Sony Plaza) in New York was a sensation. Though its architect, the legendary Philip Johnson (1906-

2005), advocated international style modernism, he chose to adorn his creation with a Chippendale pediment—clearly indicating that at the turn of this century, historical references were once again permitted.

Led by Austrian-born design veteran Ettore Sottsass, the Memphis Group, founded in Milan in 1981, embodied one of the most brilliant, albeit perverse, forms of the great stylistic appropriation that seized hold in those years. As part of that collective, Martine Bedin, Matteo Thun, Andréa Branzi, Michele de Lucchi, and others produced several epoque-making objects. They

FOLLOWING PAGES:
Julian Schnabel's loft, 1990,
New York. The artist
designed the bronze bed;
also featured is a neoclassic
marble bathtub;
large collage painting
by Julian Schnabel.

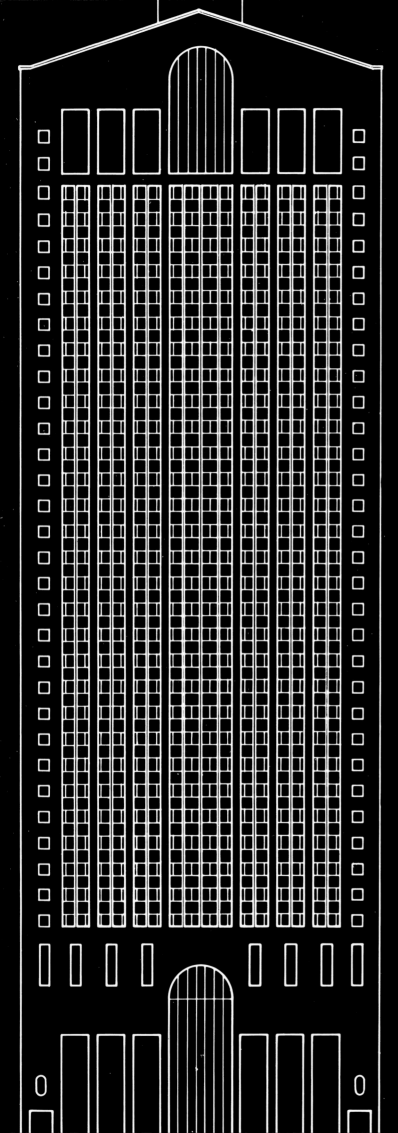

were joined in this community of spirit by Michael Graves, Hans Hollein, Shiro Kuramata, Arata Isozaki, and the proponents of the Movida in Spain—best aesthetically represented by Pedro Almodovar's film sets.

In contrast with the postmodernist melting pot, in the United States and particularly in New York City, the proponents of radical chic, alternative lifestyles, and all-out reclamation developed the high-tech style. Based on the book by Joan Kron and Susan Slesin devoted to converting lofts into living spaces, high-tech style proposed using both modern technology and industrial materials in architecture, interiors, and home furnishings.

The loft—a theatrical cross between an artist's studio and an apartment without walls—was achieved by converting semi-industrial buildings into living spaces. Inside these formerly commercial spaces, a domestic environment reconstituted beauty borrowed from institutional equipment, work-related furniture, building

Philip Johnson, project of the facade for the AT&T building in New York, 1980.

OPPOSITE: Ettore Sottsass, Libreria Carlton bookshelf covered with laminated polychrome, Memphis edition, 1981.

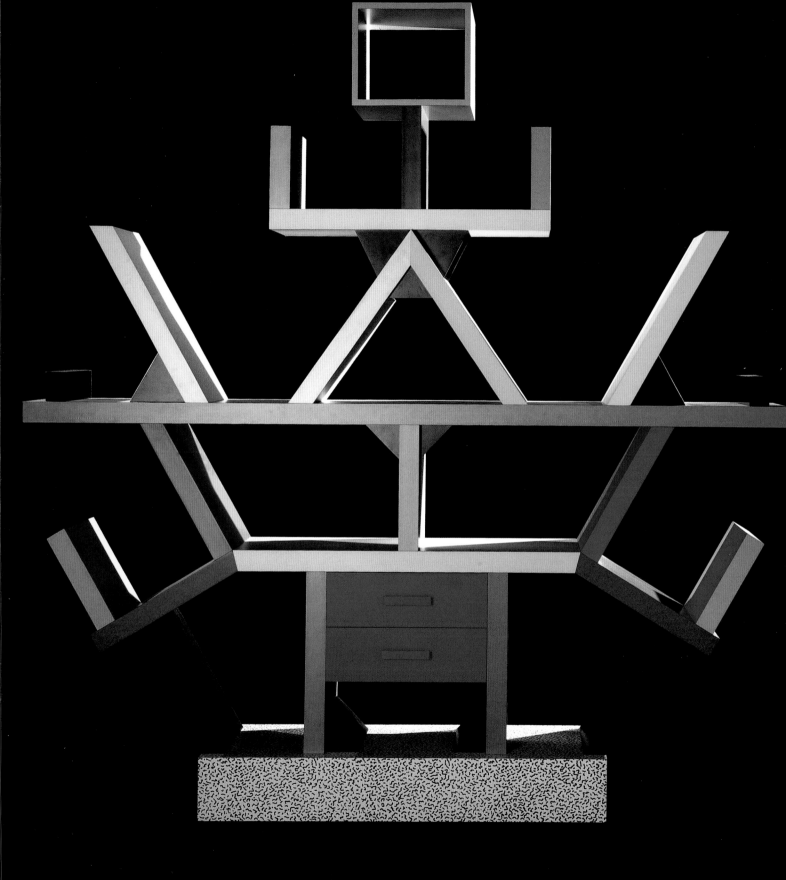

accessories, and even army surplus. Metal skylights, bolted-steel girders, unfinished bleached-wood floors, restaurant-quality kitchen equipment, hospital bathroom fixtures, rubber tiles, fluorescent tubes, neon lights, aluminum in many shapes and forms, and packing crates were some of the materials used to decorate the Yuppie home, indicating a return to eclecticism.

Above and beyond being fashionable and meeting the increasing desire for space, the loft phenomenon, which has been expanding ever since, can be largely ascribed to an economic reality.

In the latter third of the twentieth century, housing in good neighborhoods became increasingly rare; simultaneously, older, labor-intensive industries progressively abandoned the cities. In Europe, media and style moguls grabbed the ball on the rebound and adapted high-tech to their old cities. However, since their urbanism was less suited to the style, such total renewal would prove less obvious than on the other side of the Atlantic. (Despite the fact that the Pompidou Center had already familiarized people with this engineering aesthetic, which may be mainly credited to Jean Prouvé.)

OPPOSITE: **Chelsea loft of the sculptor Bernar Venet; a space that combines work and private life.**

Shiro Kuramata *How High is the Moon* chair, c. 1990.

OPPOSITE:
Tom Dixon, prototype chair "S," c. 1988.

FOLLOWING PAGES:
Donald Judd, bedroom, 1987.

A pioneer in minimalism, Donald Judd installed in his Spring Street loft, a series of neon sculptures conceived by Dan Flavin to alter the rhythm of high windows. On the wall, abstract canvas by the artist, 1963.

A warehouse atmosphere permeated decoration, and Parisan designer Andrée Putman pioneered the style. Her essential residential structures had a palette reduced to gray, beige, black, and white.

Their harmony, which was an extension of the contemporary creations of the Union des Artistes Modernes, focused on the timeless, albeit with a subtle retro feel, and was sustained by the successful reissue of chairs by the likes of Robert Mallet-Stevens, René Herbst, and Eileen Gray. Creations that enjoyed little fame in their own time, went on to become identified by many as the very essence of the 1980s.

In 1983, Putman, who was already dubbed the grande dame of style, refurbished the Morgans Hotel in New York in black and white. Her designs, and the polished photographs that were taken of them, triggered a phenomenon in the international press. Putnam's personality and influence, even more than her work, accelerated the star quality that would from then on be associated with her accessible, yet highly sophisticated decors.

A monster of design followed on the heels of Putman. Born in 1949, a perfect representative of the hip baby-boom generation, Philippe Starck began designing in the late sixties, but truly arrived on the scene in 1984, with the inauguration of Café Costes in Paris. A versatile product designer and his own best self-promoter, Starck released many of his creations as designer series. They emphasized beauty at a low cost and were mass-

produced, giving his designs a reality that perfectly reflected his generation and his vision of "good design for the masses." Starck acquired a fan base that extended from Italy to New England. When he redecorated New York's Royalton Hotel in 1988, it became an alternative to the famous Morgans.

Creative periods generally correspond with cycles of economic euphoria or elite renewal. After the industrial reclamation and the rerelease of classic modern design, the 1980s saw the appearance of a new generation of furniture and object designers, none of whom belonged to the Milanese tradition. Tom Dixon, Pascal Mourgue, Jean Nouvel, Jean Michel Wilmotte, Richard Sapper, Ron Arad, Sylvain Dubuisson, Martin Szekely, and Norman Foster were all from very different backgrounds. None had any direct relationship with the world of decoration. Nevertheless, their creations gave a leading-edge stamp to the interiors that incorporated them alongside designs from other eras and other sensibilities.

Philippe Starck,
Élysées chair,
Pompidou Center,
Paris, 1984.

Simultaneously with this redeployment of design, whose products reflected the upscale market flourishing in France, a neoprimitive movement emerged. It was described as "barbaric"—a reference to the first exhibition of the duo of Élisabeth Garouste (b. 1949) and Mattia Bonetti (b. 1953), whose Baroque, nonconformist aesthetic stunned the press, who dubbed them "the New Barbarians" in 1981. Boulder furnishings, wrought-iron chairs, animal skins, leather ties: their furniture deliberately flew in the face of all current trends. It

Philippe Starck, bar at the
Peninsula Hotel, 1992.

*A long translucent table dissects
this room located on the top floor
of the hotel. The seats are adorned
with covers printed with the faces of
the designer and his friends.*

more readily took its inspiration from Arte Povera, eighteenth-century rococo, and even prehistoric caves, as depicted in comic strips and movies.

"Our modernity is an unbroken path from all sources and all movements in history," declared the two visual artists, signifying that they operated outside of time and the modernist and post-modernist decades. In the spirit of ornamental overabundance, Garouste and Bonetti designed several iconic decors of the late eighties. The most famous and influential of these remains the fashion design house of Christian Lacroix, which opened on rue du Faubourg Saint Honoré in 1987.

At the time, postmodernism was at the end of its run. Its crea-

tions, which did not reflect any virtuosic artisanship, were copiously plagiarized. Not to mention, 1987 was also the year of a major crash on Wall Street. Along with their investors, many decorators and home decor companies took a dive. For many, it seemed the time was right for a new moderation.

Christian Liaigre was the right person at the right time. In browns, creams, and grays, using beautiful materials such as linen, silk, and wool, and polished finishes in dark wood and bronze, he refined modernism with an elegance and style reminiscent of Jean-Michel Frank in the 1940s, with a touch of Asian inspiration.

Élisabeth Garouste's and Mattia Bonetti's design of the *Trapani* console, 1997. Watercolor.

OPPOSITE: The rooms in the house of fashion designer Christian Lacroix, decorated by Garouste and Bonetti, 1987. Rue du Faubourg-Saint-Honoré, Paris.

The decorator's palette was so precise that it scarcely left room for any doubt. It was so intentionally neutral that many of his colleagues—architects in particular—did not hesitate to incorporate his essential furnishings into their own creations. With Liaigre, a new form of bourgeois classicism was born, which has since been heavily copied.

Like many stars of contemporary decoration, Liaigre became known through hotels—first with the Montalembert in Paris, then with the Mercer Hotel in SoHo, which became "the place to be" in the nineties in New York.

Liaigre's Zen style allowed people to feel transported while still relaxed and at home. Moreover, many unashamedly transferred this style to their own homes, creating a new genre: decorative understatement. Some groupings, with their dark woods and light-colored linens, taupe rugs and tawny leather, call to mind poet Henri Michaux's question: "Take away everything, nothing remains.

PRECEDING PAGES:
LEFT: Calvin Klein boutique. Paris.
RIGHT: Philippe Starck, monumental table in crystal created for the Baccarat boutique, 2004. Paris.

OPPOSITE: Christian Liaigre, Hakkasan restaurant, London, 2000.

Rooms of the Chanel house, redeveloped by Karl Lagerfeld Rue Cambon, Paris, in 2003.

Crystal chandelier by Mathias (Baccarat).

OPPOSITE: The famous multi-faceted mirrored stairwell conceived by the eponymous designer in the 1930s.

Temple of new art and design trends, David Gill's loft,
Lambeth, London, 2005.

Take away nothing, what remains?" This sums up the entire challenge of decoration, design, and fashion at the dawn of the 1990s. It was as if the century, tired of having done so much, was withdrawing into a cautious reserve and a search for inner purity that so felicitously contrasted with the turbulent outside world and the hedonistic excesses of the eighties. Man, hurried and racing around a place where he no longer perceives anything but a few hotel bars, seeks refuge.

This manner of setting up sparse environments as a precious gift would soon influence Calvin Klein in the costly decoration of his new stores. Their monastic atmosphere in turn attracted a refined clientele who appreciated pure forms. Without the store's cutting edge audiovisual equipment, one might think a minimalist apartment had just been burglarized.

Minimalism in decoration was also the logical end result of an artistic movement that had taken as its own Mies van der Rohe's injunction that "less is more." Architect John Pawson (b. 1949) takes this logic to its most extreme, eliminating practically all furnishings and the slightest trace of life.

PRECEDING PAGES:
LEFT: Loft of Didier Krentowski, host of the Kreo gallery, Paris, c. 2000.
RIGHT: Karma Rashid, living room in a country house, New York, 2005.

356

ABOVE: India Madhavi, collection house in Greenwich Village, New York, 2002.
Chair by Jean Prouvé and Bishop pedestal table by Madhavi.

FOLLOWING PAGES:
John Pawson, Catherine and John Pawson's house, London, 1999.

Conclusion

One thing that can be said about both the century of Louis XI and this third millennium is that home interiors did not—and do not—evolve much. Styles develop, overlap, boldly contradict one another, and often repeat. They are similar and always different, like home dwellers themselves. Take for example the style that accompanied Marie-Antoinette to the guillotine. It was both borrowed from her predecessor, with whom she identified, and passed down to the Empress Eugenia. The Marie-Antoinette style was later used by César Ritz for his hotels, which catered to royalty, and then was adapted to suit apartments in chic neighborhoods before traveling across the globe on Christian Dior perfume bottles.

Today, after many other metamorphoses, Louis XVI has furnished Philippe Starck with an armchair model made of transparent plastic. The style has had remarkable continuity, constantly being copied and parodied, but remaining contemporary. Louis XVI style unites and comforts the French, because it's about France through the ages. It is just how the Gothic style meets the needs of the English in every circumstance, whether for an abbey façade, a humble railway station, or even a nightclub.

Only fifty years ago, traveling into space seemed to be man's destiny. And as a result, the modern homes of the fifties and sixties were futuristic in style. After that mod-mood passed, old and worn out chic made a comeback, and antique dealers were

OPPOSITE:
Tejo Remy, *You Can't Lay Down Your Memories*, 1990. Recycled wood, maple, plastic, metal, and cardboard drawers; cotton belt.

everywhere, revisiting other twentieth-century decades up until our present time. And then, suddenly, the sixties reemerged, in the ultra-modern style adopted by the children of its original designers, who created wall-to-wall shag carpeting and lava lamps. It's a never-ending cycle!

Today a stylish interior is one that seems empty, one whose decor isn't dated, or at least doesn't seem to be. For it's easy to get lost in a game of mirrors, imitating periods of the past. In the same way, it's sometimes hard to tell the difference between a real Renaissance jewel and one designed with the same degree of care. Andrée Putman, for example, was so successful in re-issuing the little Mallet-Stevens chair in the 1980s that it has forever become associated with the "loft style" and museum cafeterias. Limited-edition furnishings designed by Aalto, Mies van der Rohe, and Herbst fetch significant prices at public auctions, despite the fact that their original models are always being copied. And so, the style of our times seems to be made up of all other styles. They're combined by decorators who work like hip DJs making original tracks from tunes written by others. Their sampling of decors—which might include, say, hanging a crystal chandelier in a high-tech kitchen—culminates in a pastiche under the guise of being new.

Even in the new millennium, interior decor continues to be guided by four distinct directions, like points of a compass. Each indicates one of four general types in which most decors can be classified. To the north is the cradle: the birth of the rustic and curiosity. It piques the interest of those nostalgic for basic living and self-sufficiency. To the south there's the eighteenth century, which remains the standard of fundamental values. To the west stands the bastion of Art Deco, with its numerous international interpretations, the summit of a modern century. It calls out to contemporary art, to the east, which is built on the rubble of the future, the clean slate of emptiness, and incessant appropriation.

These four directions are, of course, only benchmarks that help us find our way in the fairytale of styles and the hodge-podge of real life. On top of it all, there are myriad variations in decor, to which shrewd dealers attempt to put a price. Meanwhile, magazines devoted to the subject give them a time and place. The relationship between the rhythm of fashion and decor increases, especially as clothing designers develop home lines to support their "art of living" throughout the world. A full-page Versace advertisement, showing a man wearing nothing but a cloth lampshade, is, incidentally, the height of a certain kind of taste, one which no longer has any limits or boundaries. Because many decorators travel across the globe designing the same environments for a privileged few who imitate one another, there is cause to worry about a globalization of style—a phenomenon which has occurred in other fields. Hotel rooms are but one example.

What is crucial, however, is that unlike what we wear, our interior decor can meld together radically different eras, forms, and functions. Save for a John Galliano runway show, can you imagine a woman coiffed with a hennin, powdered white, girthed in garters from 1900 and kicking up her heels in cowboy boots? Many middle-class homes present this composite approach to decor without being offensive. The concept of matching sets is practically obsolete, and what remains is diversity. Each period, each find, each inheritance, adds its discordant note, and it does so without betraying a notion of unity. Our contemporaries have continued to create their own styles, using the leftovers of others. This accumulation, along with a radical stripping down, is what invents tomorrow's decor. It's like shuffling cards for a new hand: future designers will fill the pages of other books that will continue where this one has left off.

OPPOSITE: Jean-Pierre Raynaud, *Destruction of the House*. C.A.P.C., Bordeaux. See page 322 for the history of this happening.

Bibliography

André Arbus, architecte décorateur des années 40, Yvonne Brunhammer, 2003.

Antiquaires, Jean-Louis Gaillemin, Assouline, 2000.

Antonio Gaudí, Juan Jose Lahuerta, Gallimard, 1992.

Armand-Albert Rateau, Franck Olivier-Vial and François Rateau, Éditions de l'Amateur, 1996.

L'Art 1900, Maurice Rheims, A.M.G. , 1965.

L'Art de vivre, Dominique Browning, Assouline, 2003.

L'Art déco dans le monde, 1910-1939, Renaissance du livre, 2003.

L'Art décoratif en Europe (volumes 1 & 2), Citadelles, 1992.

L'Art en France sous le second Empire, Jean Darmon, RMN, 1979.

L'Art français (4 vol.), André Chastel, Flammarion, 2000.

Les Artistes décorateurs, 1900-1942, Yvonne Bruhammer and Suzanne Tise, Flammarion, 1990.

Authentic Decor, Peter Thornton, Weidenfeld and Nicolson, 2000.

Biedermeier, Angus Wilkie, Abbeville Press, 1992.

Châteaux en Suède, Haken Groth, Thames and Hudson, 1990.

Civilisation de Saint-Pétersbourg, Brigitte de Montelos and Winnie Denker, Mengès, 2001.

David Hicks : Designer, Ashley Hicks, Scriptum editions, 2003.

The Decorative Thirties, Martin Battersby, Studio Vista, 1971.

Design 1950-2000, Flammarion, 2000.

Industrial Design, Raymond Loewy, The Overlook Press, 1998.

Designer Monographs 7, Garouste et Bonetti, Verlag Form, 1996.

Destin du baroque, Germain Bazin, Hachette, 1970.

Dictionnaire de l'ameublement et de la décoration depuis le XIIIᵉ siècle jusqu'à nos jours, (volume 4), Henry Havard, Maison Quantin, 1890.

Le XVIIᵉ siècle français, Stéphane Saniel, Connaissance des arts/Hachette, 1958.

Le XVIIIᵉ siècle français, Stéphane Saniel, Connaissance des arts/Hachette, 1970.

Elsie de Wolfe : a Decorative Life, Nina Campbell and Caroline Seebohm, Panache Press/Clarkson N. Potter, Inc., 1992.

L'Égyptomanie dans l'art occidental, Jean-Marcel Humbert, ACR, 1989.

The Time and its Style, Peter Thornton, Flammarion, 1993.

Empire, Madeleine Deschamps, Abbeville Press, 1997.

Fornasetti, designer of dreams, Patrick Mauriès, Thames and Hudson, 1991.

Frank Lloyd Wright Architect, Peter Reid and Terence Riley, Museum of Modern Art, 1994.

Grammaire des arts décoratifs, Noel Riley, Patricia Bayer, Flammarion, 2004.

Gilbert Poillerat, François Baudot, Hazan, 1999.

An Illustrated History of Interior Decoration, Mario Praz, Thames and Hudson, 1994.

Histoire du design de 1940 à nos jours, Raymond Guidot, Hazan, 2004.

Horta : naissance et dépassement de l'Art nouveau, Ludion/Flammarion, 1996.

International Arts and Crafts, directed by Karen Livingstone and Linda Parry, Victoria and Albert Museum, 2005.

Jacques-Émile Ruhlmann, The Designer's Archives, Emmanuel Bréon, Flammarion, 2004.

Jean-Michel Frank, Léopold-Diego Sanchez, Éditions du Regard, 1997.

Jean Royère, Pierre-Emmanuel Martin-Vivier, Norma Éditions, 2002.

Jean Royère, décorateur à Paris, musée des Arts décoratifs/Norma éditions, 1999.

John Soane, le rêve de l'architecte, Gallimard, 2001.

Madame de Pompadour et les arts, RMN, 2002.

La Maison du XVIIIᵉ siècle en France, Pierre Verlet, Baschet and Cie, 1966.

Furniture and Interiors of the 1960s, Anne Bony, Flammarion, 2004.

Le Musée des années 30, Éditions Somogy, 1996.

L'Œil du décorateur (volumes 1 & 2), Julliard, 1963.

Les Palais du rêve, Claude Arthaud, Paris Match, 1970.

Paris 1400 : les arts sous Charles VI, Fayard, 2004.

Pierre Chareau : architecte-meublier, 1883-1950, Kenneth Frampton and Marc Vellay, Éditions du Regard, 1984.

René Herbst, Solange Goguel, Éditions du Regard, 1990.

Le Soleil et l'Étoile du Nord : la France et la Suède au XVIIIᵉ siècle, RMN/AFAA., 1994.

Russian Furniture: The Golden Age 1780-1840, Antoine Chenevière, The Vendome Press, 1988.

Starck - Mardaga, Christine Collin, Taschen, 1989.

Le Style anglais 1750-1850, Collection Connaissance des arts/Hachette, 1956.

Putman Style, Stéphane Gerschel, Assouline, 2005.

Le Style Regency, Steven Parissien, Phaidon, 2001.

The Windsor Style, Suzy Menkes, éditions du Chêne, 1987.

Les Styles, Philippe Jullian, Le Promeneur, 1992.

Tesori dalle Collezioni Medicee, Octavo, 1997.

Theo van Doesburg, painter and architect, Evert van Straaten, Gallimard, 1993.

U.A.M., l'Union des artistes modernes, Arlette Barré Despond, Éditions du Regard, 1991.

Un temps d'exubérance : les arts décoratifs sous Louis XIII et Anne d'Autriche, RMN, 2002.

La Villa Noailles, une aventure moderne, François Carrassen, Plon, 2001.

The World of Thomas Jefferson at Monticello, Abrams Susan R. Stein, 1993.

Some of the titles that are not longer available for purchase can be found at the bibliothèque des Arts décoratifs (111, rue de Rivoli, 75001 Paris).

Index

Copyrights

Acknowledgments

We would like to thank: Adam Bartos; Anne Blecksmith at the Getty Research Institute; Antonio Martinelli; Ashley Hicks; Barbara and René Stoeltie; Bildarchiv Foto Marburg; Caroline Baron at the Charleston Trust; Cécile Bouvet; Charlotte Grant at Christie's; Christian Liaigre and especially Astrid at the Clarisse Robert Press service of the Photothèque Gaud; David Gill; Deide Von Shaewen; Dolmen Ediciones; Dorothée Nourisson; Dorothy Draper Company, Inc; Elyse Hardy at the Rapho/Top agency; Eric Boman; Fabienne Grevy at the AKG agency; Francesca Alongi; François Halard; Guillaume at Laubier; Herbert Ypma; J. F. Bauret; Jacques Garcia and Melina Crisostomo; Jacques Dirand; Jean and Tom Moulin at Moulin Studio; Jean François Jaussaud and the team at Lux Production; Jean-Frédérique Schall; Jérome Lacharmoise at L'Illustration; Jill Bloomer at the Cooper Hewitt Museum; Karen Malarcan at John Pawson; Keiichi Tahara; The Andrée Putman Agency; The Artur Photo Agency; The Bridgeman Art Library Agency; The Esto Agency; The G. Dagli Orti Agency; The Keystone Agency; The Scoop Agency; The Casa Mollino team, Turin; The Georges Pompidou Center/Musée National d'Art Moderne; Lionel Dutruc at the Musée de Grenoble; Liz O'Brien; Luis Medina; Martine Baverel at the Galerie Vallois; Michael Stier, Leigh Montville, Gretchen Fenston and Diane Landers at Conde Nast Publication Inc.; Paolo de Mazio at the Galleria de Arte Moderna, and Giuseppe Schiavinotto; Pascal Hinous; Peter Reed; Pierrick Jean the RMN agency; Rachel Lloyd at the Victoria and Albert Museum; Randy Juster; Sandra Wiskaria at the Metropolitan Museum of Art; Scala Archives; Baccarat Press service; Calvin Klein Press service; Philip Starck Press service; Shirley Mellul, Caroline Berton and Michel Zaquin at Editions Conde Nast S.A.; The Interior Archive; Bernard Ladoux; Valérie Lantignac at the CAPC of Bordeaux; Véronique Garrique at the ADAGP; Vincent Knapp; Yukio Futagawa.